Advance Praise

This is the journey of a woman resented by her father for merely being born. Determined to win love, Gloria graduated valedictorian of her class. She was an adventurous world traveler and later devoted all her time caring for abandoned kittens, often sacrificing her own needs. She placed her trust in animals, not people. She had a brilliant mind and spirit but could be bitter and brutally honest. Torn by dementia at the end, you are left to wonder if she found salvation in the loving arms of Jesus Christ. I am so thankful to have shared a small portion of her journey. I always loved her dearly.

– Janice Holladay, Calhoun County Humane Society

To try and write out the content of someone's life, of a time in both world history and family history, is a monumental task. After reading *Not How It Was Supposed to Be*, as a member of Gloria's family I find myself nearly broken in a way. So thankful and happy for the ending, but as much as I knew from my mom and her generation, and witnessed myself, reading it is really hard. I find myself flooded with all the confusion, lack of understanding, and "why" of all the parts of my own upbringing that I've never fully processed either.

– James Menke, Gloria's first cousin once removed

It's been said that "a mind is a terrible thing to waste," but in this case it may be, "a mind is a terrible thing to lose." Lewy body dementia becomes a bad dream from which you never wake. This book has real-life experiences of my friend, and the pain and anguish she and her mother encountered with this tormenting disease. And with this story, may more awareness give rise to further research, because we still have a long, long way to go.

– Linda Marie Mabry-Meyer, RN, BSN

This is a story I view as a mysterious and complex piece of my life. Until the last few days of her journey, Gran's life stirred feelings of anger, resentment, and a general degree of confusion for me. I did not have the opportunity to know her well, but I do know what I view as the most important part of her story. The home that a child is raised in has impacts that never fade and seem to go in one of two directions. You either live a life that reflects those negative aspects or find the ability to overcome it and shape the next generation in complete contrast to what you knew. I am thankful my mother was able to choose the latter of the two. Most importantly this story represents the ultimate chance at redemption through the grace of God, forgiveness for a life lived.

– Luke Crabtree, Gloria's Grandson

Not How It Was Supposed to Be

Not How It Was Supposed to Be

Seasons of Loss and Shadows of Grace in the Journey with Lewy Body Dementia

ALLISON CRABTREE

NOT HOW IT WAS SUPPOSED TO BE
Seasons of Loss and Shadows of Grace in the Journey with Lewy Body Dementia

Copyright © 2025 by Allison Crabtree

All rights reserved. No part of this book may be reproduced, distributed, or transmitted in any form or by any means, including photocopying, recording, or other electronic or mechanical methods, without the written permission from the publisher or author, except as permitted by US copyright law or in the case of brief quotations embodied in a book review.

Disclaimer: Although the publisher and the author have made every effort to ensure that the information in this book was correct at press time and while this publication is designed to provide accurate information in regard to the subject matter covered, the publisher and the author assume no responsibility for errors, inaccuracies, omissions, or any other inconsistencies herein and hereby disclaim any liability to any party for any loss, damage, or disruption caused by errors or omissions, whether such errors or omissions result from negligence, accident, or any other cause.

Unless otherwise noted, scripture quotations are from the Revised Standard Version of the Bible, copyright © 1946, 1952, and 1971 National Council of the Churches of Christ in the United States of America. Used by permission. All rights reserved worldwide.

Cover Design by Abigael Elliott
Interior Layout and Design by Alice Briggs
Editorial Team: Traci Matt, Ginny Glass, Becca Blackburn, Kiska Carr

ISBN:
979-8-89165-247-7 *Paperback*
979-8-89165-248-4 *Hardback*
979-8-89165-246-0 *ebook*

Published by:
Streamline Books
Kansas City, MO
streamlinebookspublishing.com

Dedication

To my sons, John, Paul, and Luke. Words cannot express how very blessed and proud I am to be your mom. Your father and I love you so very much. Watching you grow into godly men, accomplishing so many impressive things, is our greatest joy. My hope is that this book provides you with some understanding of our family dynamics and gives your children a window into their legacy.

Family is everything.

Gran loved you very much.

Contents

Preface xiii
Introduction. xix
    Not Good Enough xxi
    Sign Me Up. xxiii

Chapter 1: The Tanners 1
    The Wrong Time. 2
    The Home Place 4
    A Legacy of Faith and Despair. 6
    Ronnie 9

Chapter 2: Gloria 15
    To Have and To Hold 17
    Dad. 20
    Making a Home 21

Chapter 3: Texas Living 25
    Shadows of the Past. 26
    Off to College Station 28
    Adulting 33
    A Tale of Two Religions. 35

Chapter 4: Twilight Gathers 39
Foxholes and Deathbeds 41
Her Babies. 44
My Babies 46
Not How We Do Things 48
Dress Rehearsal 50

Chapter 5: What Is Happening? 55
The Keys 58
Fitting Together Puzzle Pieces 60

Chapter 6: The Diagnosis 67
I Cannot Live Like This 68
The Lists 69
That Horrible Wednesday 71

Chapter 7: Too Soon 77
A New Normal 79
The Storage Container 81

Chapter 8: The Final Days 87
The Long Drive 89
Day Two 90
Day Three 92
Day Four 93
Day Five 94
Day Seven 97
Day Eight 98
Day Nine 99
The Lord's Day 99

Epilogue 103
Acknowledgments 107
About the Author 109

Preface

But O for the touch of a vanished hand, and the sound of a voice that is still!

—*Alfred, Lord Tennyson*

MY HUSBAND ROUNDED the corner and then stepped back when I looked up, eyes brimming with tears, as I cradled a box of my mother's things in my lap.

"I thought you had already worked through all this," Doug said not unkindly.

"I thought so too."

More than four years after my mother, Gloria Tanner Tucker Saylor, had succumbed to the ravages of Lewy body dementia, a progressive condition that presents symptoms similar to Parkinson's disease, there I sat, deep in the weeds of her story. Some of those weeds were sharp, drawing blood, some left behind annoying burrs in my socks, and a few even entangled me, intent on stopping forward progress. But, like a sweeping field of Queen Anne's lace or the delicate spores of the dandelion, there was also an undeniable beauty inherent to the process.

The unfolding of her story has also been, surprisingly, the unfolding of mine. As much as I wanted to discover heretofore unknown motivations for her hurtful behavior and assure myself and my boys that she loved us with all her heart, I feared the clues she left behind would lead to nothing but dead ends. Heartache. But as I read, processed, and wrote, the shadows of her life became ever so slightly clearer, like an antique mirror that has been dusted and polished yet still remains cloudy and even black in spots where the silver has worn away. Moreover, as time went on, I could see my own face reflected in the mirror as well.

One of the final conversations between Mother and me took place in a dark, sterile hospital room as she vacillated between hallucinations and unquestionable lucidity. This was a moment of clarity for her, but it left me confused:

"Finish the book. Get it published," the exchange began, and she reached for me as if to emphasize the importance of the message. I could tell by the sharp focus of her eyes and determined tone of her voice that she was drawing from the dwindling well of her sanity.

"What? What book, Mother?"

"Finish the book. Get it published."

"What are you talking about? I'm not writing a book."

"Finish the book. Get it published."

"All right, Mom. I will finish the book and get it published. I promise."

She laid back, slowly bobbing her head, and closed her eyes as the urgent moment faded away.

This side of heaven I will never know exactly what she had envisioned as "the book," but after the fog of her suffering and death had been burned away by the passage of time, I remembered my promise and began to consider what in the world she had been talking about. All indicators pointed to telling the story of a woman born at the wrong point in history, choked nearly to death by the patriarchal social structure she could not escape, yet driven to excellence in all she was allowed to attempt.

Rest assured this is not a sanitized tribute designed to solidify selective memories or nominate her for sainthood. My mother's journey was anything but pristine and worthy of emulation. Yet she loved and was loved, served and was served, and, in the end, allowed God to strip her of the unworthiness and false pride that had plagued her since the first time her daddy looked upon her with contempt.

A word of advice to anyone endeavoring to weave together the life story of a loved one who has passed: Be prepared for the heavy emotional toll that will be extracted from your heart and soul during the process. Each moment of research and mulling the circumstances of Mother's life, grasping at details in an attempt to make sense of the truth before me, required mental gymnastics and every ounce of strength I could conjure. It was as if the very threads of my spirit were stretched to their ultimate tensile strength in order to make sense of the woman who had given me life.

My editor took on the role of a surrogate therapist as we sifted through papers and memories, often pushing me to open doors to dark closets I would rather ignore. Every recollection came with a heavy dose of introspection. Things I can't remember and those I wish I couldn't. Blank spaces in memory and unanswerable questions about the "why" in countless situations.

You see, as I stepped into adulthood, I realized that my mother and I did not have what anyone would call a close relationship. Quite the opposite was true. Even though I had no siblings, for reasons I understand better now than ever but will never truly grasp, she expressed no desire to develop a substantial mother-daughter bond—physical, emotional, or particularly spiritual. In the place of a familial connection, she built a wall, brick by brick, every time I questioned her or made a choice she did not approve of. And that, unfortunately, happened often.

As a child, I had no idea that our relationship was abnormal. From my vantage point, she was an exceptional mother, sewing my clothing with panache, cultivating beautiful flowers and vegetables, taking me to church every week, and requiring excellence from me in school and all aspects of our daily life. Yet, as I grew older and ventured from the nest, my eyes were opened to our dysfunction. Primarily, there was a fundamental lack of affection. Our home was one without hugs and attagirls, ruffled hair and loving words. She was proud of me and told me often, but every crumb of affirmation came with a long string attached. I honestly don't remember making an independent decision for myself until the first day I stepped onto a university campus. My schedule, clothing, interests, and friends were all determined by her whims. The stark irony was that she did not care to invest herself in anything more than the surface aspects of my life. For emotional and spiritual advice, comfort, and encouragement, I was forced to turn elsewhere.

One thing was for certain: You never had to wonder what Mother was thinking about you. Opinions—solicited or unsolicited—were things she had a seemingly uncontrollable need to share. Even as an adult, making any sort of decision without her permission meant shouldering the inevitable criticism and disapproval. She did not like my choice of a mate. She was not supportive when I became pregnant the first time. In fact, she pitied me, inventorying the drawbacks of starting a family: late-night feedings, spit-up, and, most importantly, the yielding of any claim I had on my own dreams. There were no heartfelt conversations about stretch marks and layettes, christenings and daycare, and she certainly did not come to help when her newborn grandson made his appearance. She taught me to be tough and self-sufficient. And I was.

I am.

But how do you deal with the pain of your mother's disdain when your friend gushes about how excited hers is to become a grandmother? How do you explain to three small boys why only their father's parents ever come to grandparents' day at school? What do you say when the tender-hearted preschooler looks up, hesitating before running to Gran for a hug? Why she doesn't come to their games or ever take care of them when Mommy and Daddy are away? They may have been young, but they understood that even though she did love them, she had no interest in being a grandmother. She was too busy living her life of passionate service to strangers and animals. She logged hours with the local pet rescue operation and sometimes deprived herself so her house full of felines thrived. Her eyes would light up, talking about her latest trip to South America, where she spotted the elusive whatever-it's-called bird, but she could not make time to attend her grandsons' games or concerts. Everything Mother took on for her own interests, she did with extreme conviction. She could have been the world's best grandmother. I still scratch my head over this contradiction—this grievous loss for all of us.

As real as our dysfunction was, my mother was an amazing woman—a singular human being. Raised in an era and domestic structure where females were powerless and subservient, she charted a course of self-fulfillment and independence worthy of a true adventuress. Her journey from pregnant teen to animal welfare volunteer, world traveler, and gardener extraordinaire was something to behold. Memories of her exceptional musical talent echo in my mind, chords of hymns filling the church as her hands and feet moved ceaselessly on the pipe organ.

The last harrowing years and months of her life, I could not stop wishing, praying, even demanding that God would tear down that damn brick wall so we could finally find comfort in each other's presence. He was gracious to give me a few peepholes, scattered glimpses into what motivated her to make the choices she did, but the wall, unfortunately, remained. Only the power of Jesus Christ's sacrifice gives me the hope that Mother and I will someday be able to shape a healthy relationship in the shadow of God's glorious throne.

So, for the sake of my boys and myself, for those with Lewy body dementia and their loved ones and caregivers, for those struggling with faith and the hereafter, here is the story of Gloria Saylor. Her journey, a maddening and confusing contradiction of selfishness and service, standoffishness and love, culminating, thankfully, with eternal hope in Christ Jesus.

So whether what you hold in your hand is the result of the dementia-induced rambling of an old woman on her deathbed or an inspired vision from heaven above, I have finished the book.

Mother, it's done. I know you are proud.

Introduction

*At the acceptable time I have listened to you, and
helped you on the day of salvation.*

—2 Corinthians 6:2a

WE'RE SOME OF *the lucky ones*, I mused, bending over to fluff my mother's pillow and wipe her brow for the hundredth time. The muted television screen scrolled the latest updates, "US Death Toll Nears 100,000," "Unemployment Highest Since Great Depression," "Fauci Warns Against Premature Reopening," "Healthcare Workers Help Family Members Say Goodbyes Via Facetime." Yet there we were, Mother and I, together.

Double-masked and overtasked, nurses and aides peeked frequently into the dark room to check on us, knowing there was little they could do to halt the ravages of the disease that was stripping, moment by moment and layer by layer, my mom's sanity and dignity. When they approached, donning masks, goggles, gloves, and other protective gear, she would panic. That was no surprise, considering how horrifying they must have appeared to a mind that tended toward the hallucinations inherent to her condition.

The incessant beeping of the morphine drip was punctuated by Mother's nonstop, nonsensical babbling. The disease's classic end stage had her in its grip with constant anxiety and tension. In her mind's eye, an unending list of life tasks yet to be completed stretched beyond the horizon. Sleep eluded her as she dug in the phantom garden and packed invisible boxes, filling unseen bowls with cat food and gripping an imaginary steering wheel like a toddler playing a game. Several times, she asked for my assistance, and, taking the advice of dementia experts, I entered her world and agreed to help. Then, when I didn't jump up immediately to begin my assigned task, she would admonish, "Get moving. We've got to get this done! Let's get going!"

At one point, I tried this approach to calm her: "You don't have to work anymore, Mom. You've done it all, and you've done it well."

Always one to see through insincere attempts at placation, she provided one of many moments of levity: "Bullshit."

It was early May 2020, a time when other families were gathered around bouquet-laden tables, cautiously celebrating the joys of maternal instinct for Mother's Day in the middle of a pandemic. Because of my mom's rapidly declining health, Doug and I were being denied one of those glorious family gatherings with our three sons and their families, which now included two precious grandbabies. Although I wouldn't wish anyone to die alone and I was grateful to the doctors and hospital staff for allowing me access, the selfish side of me, honestly, was pretty irritated about the inconvenience of Mother's timing. She would be the first to admit she hadn't been a great mother and an even less satisfactory grandmother, and the irony of the situation was not lost on either of us. I had to keep reminding myself how horrible I would feel if she died alone, as so many around us were doing every day.

Crippled by exhaustion, anger, and grief, I struggled to pray. After all, decades of intercession for my mother had a history of dissolving into the ether, unanswered. She and I had had countless discussions about faith and eternity, and nothing but skepticism, criticism, and sarcasm ever resulted.

Our shared Lutheran background did not put forth any teaching about the need for a personal connection with Christ. Ours was a religion based on symbolism, ritual, and leaning into a cultural heritage of Christianity. As I grew older and moved beyond the confines of traditional Protestantism, I realized going through the motions of church attendance and communion was not what Jesus meant when he said in John 4:16, "I am the way, the truth, and the life; no one comes to the Father, but by me." God graciously revealed my need for a relationship with Jesus Christ through the Holy Spirit's process of repentance, acceptance, and baptism.

Mother was not impressed.

Not Good Enough

I thought about the last conversation we had regarding her eternal destiny, which resulted, once again, in a stalemate. We had been driving home from one of her many medical appointments, and Mother started talking about her dear friend Juaniece, a true angel on earth who showed up every day after my mom moved to the nursing home, often toting supplies and always delivering encouragement. Juaniece made it possible for Mother to keep her local connections, and I never had to worry about any part of her care being neglected because I was hundreds of miles away.

But that day, for some reason, Mother had been irritated with her. "I love Juaniece, but I just get so tired of her. All she does is talk about her faith and her God and how she just knows that when she dies, she's going to go to heaven. I don't understand how anybody thinks they can know that."

OK, Lord, help me once again, I prayed before responding, carefully keeping my eyes on the road: "Oh, Mother, we can all take hold of the promise of eternal life with God. That's exactly what Christ provided for us when he died on the cross. We all have a path to salvation and the peace of knowing we can go to heaven."

She huffed in response to the familiar message, and in my peripheral vision, I could see her crossing her arms and looking out her window at the passing Texas landscape before she replied softly, "I'm just not that good of a person."

"Mother, none of us are. That's the point."

I went on as the Lord gave me the words to remind her that no one is worthy of spending eternity with a perfect God. No one can do enough good to earn their way to heaven. In Luke 23, we see that the thief on the cross next to Jesus was assured a place in paradise simply by believing that the Lord took the penalty for his sins. This man died in unspeakable pain, but when he opened his eyes, he was with Jesus.

We sat in silence the rest of the drive. That day, the door cracked open, but the turmoil of the following months provided more than enough noise to drown out any thoughts of changing her stance on faith. She had no path for forgiveness that I could see at that point. Even though a small flame of hope remained within me, my desire to avoid thinking about the inevitable heartbreak of a very final goodbye kept me from bringing it up again. I prayed for opportunities to talk about it once more, but they just did not materialize. It was heavy on my heart that she was dying, but I didn't know how to get through to her.

Sign Me Up

As her disease progressed, robbing my mother of memories and basic cognitive function, I knew her days were limited. By the time I sat at her side that day in the hospital, even though she still had moments of clarity, I wondered if it was too late for her soul. Was her brain too addled to make a choice for faith in Christ? Would the antipsychotic meds she was on take away her ability to make a conscious choice that would be acceptable at the pearly gates? Did there come a point where she was lost, even before she took her final breath?

The day wore on, and Mother's anxiety spiked. She tossed and turned, moaning and mumbling, every spasm and incomprehensible word punctuated with conviction. She never did anything without complete dedication, and it appeared her final days would play out with her signature intensity.

That's when it started. The counting. She went rigid with her eyes fixed on the ceiling. "OK, what are we doing now?" I asked as I jumped up in anticipation of another severe bout of agitation. Based on the negative energy crackling around her, this promised to be a doozy.

At first, I thought she was looking at me, but then I realized she was focused on the ceiling, her eyes clear and moving along as she began, "One. Two. Three. Four…" She was definitely seeing something that I couldn't. Were there spiders or cracks up there she was hyper-focused on? "Five. Six. Seven. Eight…"

Now, I hate to admit it, but my first thought was to hold a little pity party for myself. How long were we going to have to do this? Couldn't she just stop and take a nap, for heaven's sake? I sure needed one. "Nine. Ten. Eleven. Twelve…"

After several minutes, I asked, "Mom, what are you counting?" That snapped her out of it. She jerked her head around, glaring at me, and cried out with reproach.

"He's not here!"

Again, I played along, "Mom, who are you talking about? Who's not here?"

"*Your Jesus*! He's not here! He's. Not. Here!"

At that moment, despite the obstacles of exhaustion and selfish thoughts, the Lord was able to finally get through to me. It was as if a switch had been flipped, and I could sense the battle between good and evil going on in that room—a skirmish for my mother's very soul. Although I couldn't see them as she could, I fully believe she had been counting demons sent to torment her. There were creatures from hell endeavoring to keep her soul ensnared in its pride and doubt. To taunt her, day and night, with thoughts that she was not worthy of God's love and forgiveness. That the God-man who had hung on the cross had no desire to save her. And whether there was literally an invisible field of combat in that room or she was simply giving into the hallucinations, I realized it was her last chance.

Because I knew Jesus, *my Jesus*, was indeed there.

"Mom, can you hear me? Do you know I'm here?"

"Yes," she replied, her eyes still wide with fear. At this point, with tears streaming down my face, I fought back the flashes of inadequacy when I considered the eloquent biblical message some would be able to provide this woman in what may have been her final moments of clear thinking. I was just bumbling along, but God gave me the words.

"Mom, do you understand that Jesus loves you, and he died for your sins so that you could have life ever after with him?" The silence stretched on longer than I was comfortable with as she carefully considered my proposition. God's proposition.

"Yes."

"Do you want that?"

"Yes!" she shouted. "Sign me up!"

Never had more beautiful words fallen on my ears.

I let out a breath I didn't realize I'd been holding and looked up at that ceiling, grinning like the Cheshire cat. "God, that's as good as you're gonna get."

CHAPTER 1
The Tanners

No man is an island, Entire of itself.

—*John Donne*

IN THAT SAME hospital in Port Lavaca, Texas, a lifetime away, a green-eyed baby girl was born squalling on a sultry September day. The year was 1941, and Lillie Pauline Jaster Tanner and Ralph Roy Tanner welcomed their first child.

Planet Earth at that time was on the cusp of its greatest conflict to date, with mere weeks before the day of infamy would descend upon the United States. Women had the right to vote, of course, but not the right to do much else without a nod from the men in their lives. Although they were joining the workforce in greater numbers while men were being deployed in defense of freedom, these Rosie the Riveters knew they would be expected to gracefully bow out and return to their homemaking duties once soldiers returned from war. Rosie would certainly never take a place of authority above any male in need of a job.

Normal American life remained truly Victorian in many ways. Children were to be seen and not heard. Male children were more highly valued than little girls. Men treated their wives and children in any way they saw fit, with impunity. Some were decent heads of household—others were not.

As the Tanners bundled their baby, Gloria, up for her journey home that September, they seemed like any other average, middle-class little family. Perhaps they stopped at the store for a gallon of milk or waved to the postman making his rounds. Lillie and Ralph may have even noticed the swirling clouds blowing off the gulf as portents of a hurricane that would eventually cause tremendous death and destruction. Unfortunately, a storm of cruelty and terror at the Tanner home was also brewing.

The Wrong Time

My mother, Gloria, was simply born at the wrong point on the human timeline. Now, don't get me wrong. I do believe that the good Lord has a perfect plan for our lives, but it would have been much less frustrating for her if she had come of age in the days of female Supreme Court judges and surgeons. She was always ready to take on the world and possessed the talent and temperament to do so, but sadly, the world wasn't interested.

Based on the memories she shared and things I gleaned from others, her father was deeply disappointed that she had not been born a male. For whatever reason, a man-child was the desire of his heart, and he could not be bothered to become attached to a daughter. She was simply dispensable, a bother, and he used every opportunity to remind her he would rather have had a son. The insidious rot of emotional impotence transferred easily from his generation to hers.

I have no reason to believe that Mother suffered as some did coming out of the Great Depression—her home was secure in terms of food, access to education and health care, and ties to a heritage of church involvement. She had a loving mother and extended family. I do have reason to believe that she was denied some of the fundamental rights of a child: unconditional love and the filling of the emotional cup that only a father can provide a daughter. The protection and advocacy that her mother had neither the resources nor training to provide to her children.

As I'm sure Dr. Freud would agree, it was Mother's battle for attention and acceptance (she surely gave up expecting fatherly love before she even realized what it was) that drew the baseline of her personality. In a home where floors were strewn with proverbial eggshells, she seized control of what she could by developing what we might call obsessive-compulsive tendencies. As my husband put it in more gentlemanly Texas-like terms, she did everything with conviction. From schoolwork to musical accomplishments to needlework to gardening, if she was taking it on, it was to be done with perfection. Recently, I had some of her cross-stitch work reframed to hang in my home, and it reminded me how excellence was a byword with her. She used the tightest fabric, the tiniest stitches, and every thread was pulled to an exact tautness. She poured all of herself into these projects. They are stunningly beautiful and a lovely legacy that I treasure.

Unfortunately, for the most part, relationships, temporal or spiritual, had no place in her world. She had absolutely zero conviction about connections, interaction with, or reliance on anyone or anything other than herself.

In response to her father's disdain and mother's energy being burned up in self-preservation, Gloria Tanner determined to live life, in opposition to John Donne's iconic wisdom, as an island indeed.

The Home Place

Lillie Tanner, my maternal grandmother, Maw-Maw, lived a hard life characterized by humility and frugality. Born in 1918 on the heels of World War I, she survived World War II, the Great Depression, the Cold War, the Vietnam and Korean "conflicts," and all the horrors and stressors that come with watching the world burn.

The daughter of German immigrant Fritz Jaster, who achieved the American dream of owning a farm out on the Texas Gulf Coast's Seadrift Highway, Maw-Maw was one of seven children. I think we tend to glamorize that period in time, the days of independent self-reliance, but there was nothing glamorous about the Jaster home. To say Maw-Maw was raised in a patriarchal, authoritarian household would be a vast understatement. She probably never realized there was any other family dynamic possible.

As a white male landowner, Maw-Maw's father, who I called Grandpa even though he was my great-grandpa, took seriously his role as lord of their little kingdom, ruling with an iron fist both literally and figuratively. He was a hard man, but as I reflect on his early life—leaving home as a toddler and being thrust into a new culture, new language, and new environment—it's hard to imagine how he would turn out otherwise.

Mother loved to visit her grandparents at the "home place" when she was a child. No doubt that was where her obsession with the outdoors and animals took root. She would gather eggs and catch the chickens on butchering day, Grandpa stationed at the chopping block, followed by the women putting together the best fried chicken dinner imaginable. Mother and I both struggled with this bloody process, but at the time, we didn't have the luxury of considering the ethical aspects of eating what you had just killed. It's simply how things worked on the farm—a way of survival. And the chicken was delicious.

Mother helped prune berry vines and fruit trees. She shucked corn—so much corn—and snapped beans. When the work was done, I can picture her stealing away to the barn loft with a book and a lapful of kittens, marveling at the swallows dancing in the rafters, and disappearing into another world until the dinner bell rang.

The rite of passage for every child at the home place was the taunting of Grandpa's Brahman bull. Although some family stories tend to become caricatures of the actual events, both Mother's generation and mine cheated death by gathering around the pen, hurling taunts and insults until the two-thousand-pound frame came snorting barreling toward the brave tribute, forced to run for their life and dive under the fence to the cheers of young onlookers. It was always the highlight of our visit.

As I grew up in the '60s and '70s, we lived close by and visited that farm year after year, playing dominoes with Grandpa every week in the summer, harvesting bountiful crops from the garden, and gathering around the tree while someone read the Luke 2 Christmas story from the cumbersome family Bible. Grandma had died when I was a baby, but two grown great aunties and a great uncle remained on the farm, even when they were well past courting age. Each one had a role to play in the care and keeping of their father and the home place. Uncle Louis did the heavy lifting of the farm work, Aunt Lula did all the cooking, and Aunt Selma tended the vegetable and flower gardens. Each had their little spot in the circle of life on the family farm.

It was an honor to be chosen to help Aunt Selma gather eggs, carefully navigating annoyed chickens and the threat of chicken snakes. I loved mucking through the mud, basket in hand, to hunt for eggs. In addition to being a key ingredient in almost every meal, they would take them to town every Wednesday to sell, and not every great-niece or -nephew was deemed trustworthy enough to assist with this important task.

When it occurred to me that perhaps they should be getting married and moving on, I asked my mother why they were not. She explained that Grandpa simply wouldn't allow it. From time to time, if they became interested in someone, he would intervene to stop any romantic interests. Maybe it was just the mindset of that era, maybe it was outright selfishness, but he reasoned that those children were needed to help work at the home place. To care for their aging father. Although Grandpa never had any retirement plans, his diabetes eventually caused the amputation of both legs at the knee. Yet he would insist on wheeling out to the garden, hoe in hand. He pictured himself as independent, but he was not. He required assistance. It was the duty of his children to keep the home place going. This was not some Hallmark movie where true love would come from an unexpected source and save the day; his children had no other options. So they stayed.

Maw-Maw, being one of the older daughters, was given an opportunity to escape, although she moved just down the road when she married Ralph Tanner, my Paw-Paw. She must have dreamed it would be such a relief to slip out from under her father's oppressive spirit. She yearned for love and believed her fiancé's flattery and promises, but it was not to be. As she later wrote, "I only heard love before, not after we were married."

A Legacy of Faith and Despair

Mother's family had a deep foundation in the Lutheran church, owing, presumably, to the fact her grandfather was German. There was only one Lutheran congregation in Port Lavaca when I was young, and we attended like clockwork each week as an extended family, observing the sacred rituals and reciting endless creeds and scriptures attempting to tie daily lives to the heavenly realm. The aunties would sing in the choir, and Mother would stoically take her place at the organ while I fidgeted on the pew next to Maw-Maw and Paw-Paw.

For Maw-Maw, warming a church pew every Sunday was not enough. Somehow in the midst of all that repetition and rubber-stamping, she discovered what Martin Luther had been trying to get across: The essential part of faith is a personal relationship with the creator through Jesus Christ. That's how Maw-Maw was different. She had that relationship and talked about it whenever the opportunity arose. She fed her faith during the week by listening to preachers on the airwaves and poring over Bible studies. She put her commitment to Christ into action through church sewing circles and benevolence projects. Jesus consumed her life, but tragically, that zeal became repellant to my mother.

Of course, I can only speculate, but it's clear Mother had things going on in her life that she realized were questionable in God's economy. No one likes to sit under constant criticism. I remember a time or two commenting about a biblical principle, and Mother's response was, "You can't take the Bible literally. It's not intended to be a literal interpretation; it's just a guide." How she gleaned that from years of listening to Lutheran pastors and ageless hymns is beyond me. However, I kept my mouth shut because, when Mother thought she was right, it was not worth trying to convince her otherwise. It didn't take a genius to see that one hundred percent of her skepticism came from her father. One hundred percent. Yet Maw-Maw was unrelenting.

One of my most vivid memories of Maw-Maw is her open Bible, sitting either on an end table or on her little stool, beside it, her daily devotional booklet and ubiquitous red pencil. I was young and foolish then and didn't understand or appreciate the love she had for Jesus. I'm ashamed to admit, taking cues from my mother, I often tired of Maw-Maw talking so openly about God as if he were right there with us. Now I know he most certainly was. What I wouldn't give to visit with her just one more time about her Lord and the strength and shades of joy he infused in her tragic and often monochrome life.

Maw-Maw knew both the greatest delights and the deepest sorrow any mother could face. She left behind a spiral notebook with precious glimpses into her faith and grief. This collection of snipped articles, poems, and Bible verses provided enough light to illuminate the next step of her often-shrouded path. Treasured messages of God's providence and provision were carefully glued to the pages one by one. The twenty-third Psalm, twentieth-century Christian anthem "Footprints in the Sand," special entries from the *Our Daily Bread* devotional, and lyrics from classic hymns all sang out themes of comfort, eternal hope, and, interestingly, love and forgiveness. It appears a mixture of words she relished and wisdom she prayed someone would discover and take to heart after she was gone. Perhaps she had my stubborn mother or harsh Paw-Paw in mind. Perhaps it was me.

Whether my mother ever read through the precious notes, I don't know. But there is no doubt that the sweet fragrance of Maw-Maw's prayers for her daughter never stopped ascending to the Lord's throne in heaven.

Her "confirmation verse" was Matthew 28:20b (KJV): "Lo, I am with you always, even unto the end of the world."

One other of Maw-Maw's writings that remains is not so comforting. As I dug faithfully through family papers, the last thing I expected to see was a manifesto of Maw-Maw's literal love-hate relationship with her husband. Reading her stark revelations, in the form of a handwritten letter to my mother, was like taking physical blow after blow. It took me some time to recover. I truly wish I had never found it. Because I have memories of Maw-Maw standing fearfully at the window, ready to get Paw-Paw's hot lunch on the table the minute his car rounded the curve on the highway, the intensity of dysfunction was not a complete surprise. But it was a gut punch.

The picture of a classic abuser jumped from the pages as she recounted her husband's false accusations, physical harm, intimidation, gaslighting, and even threats of murder. "All I ever did was plead with him not to be mad. 'I'm sorry,' I'd say for everything that he thought I did... I used the word *sorry* more than any word I ever used in my life to him. I was scared of him," she wrote in what appears to be an attempt to explain to her daughter why they lived the way they did. Why his attempts to turn my mother against her was just another "evil thing" he did.

"How I hated him," one sentence declares. "All I heard from him was all the boys I wanted to marry, and I hated him. Love never came up. Oh, Lord, what a good life we could have had."

Further down, she backpedals. "No, I never hated him... Oh, yes, I learned how a sick person is, the hard way. I never claimed to be perfect. I always told him there was only one Jesus... I do love you."

The cherry on top of the heartbreaking letter was a note my mom had written to me, I'm assuming as she put the letter in a box, knowing someday I would find it: *I don't remember when she wrote this, but it is so, so sad.*

Digging into this dark closet was a difficult task, but it's clear that those ugly things we wish weren't there help us understand better why people become who they are. It made me sad and mad, but in the end, it drew me closer to forgiveness.

Ronnie

One day, when little Gloria was nine years old, she learned a thrilling secret: She was going to become a big sister. I can imagine her crocheting booties and preparing to share her toys with a new sibling, welcoming a confidante and ally into her chaotic world. Nurturing expectations of giving and receiving unconditional love. However, when Ralph Tanner learned his new child was a son, Mother's life became even more of a living hell. On a chilly day in September of 1950, Ronald Tanner's entrance into the world eclipsed what remaining light his big sister had left in her spirit. From that point on, life was all about Ralph and his son. "My boy" became the byword of the house.

Ronnie was smart, thriving off the attention of his father and taking advantage of being the golden boy at every opportunity. I adored him and remember how I enjoyed hanging around listening to records and hearing all the things teenagers like to brag about to their younger relatives. He learned the lesson well from his father that his mother did not deserve an ounce of respect, and that bothered me. One time, I actually worked up the courage to reprimand him: "You need to be nicer to your mother," because I just adored her.

Ronnie earned college scholarships and graduated magna cum laude with a master's degree in secondary education, but for some reason, he could not land a job, so he enlisted in the navy. Here's where things get tricky when recreating family history based on the best a journalist could do at the time. The local gossip column says Ralph Tanner's son came home on leave from the navy, but I know that is not true. He had been discharged due to failing a psychological analysis. He was unstable, with a range of mental health issues, not the least of which was obsessive-compulsive disorder, but Paw-Paw was too embarrassed to let him seek treatment.

During his "leave," Ronnie spent his days lying around the house, drowning under the incessant demands of his father to get a job. *What a disappointment you have turned out to be. What an embarrassment. Get your act together, for God's sake.* Ronnie became so distraught that he told one family member if he could figure out a way to kill himself without leaving a mess for his mother, he would do it.

One day, Ronnie had a job interview in Victoria, a town about thirty miles from home. Newspaper accounts detail that on his way back, he was involved in a head-on collision and then struck from behind by an oil field rig. I vividly remember being called out of my high school physics class by the principal. "There's been an accident…" he began. Those four words that make your blood run cold.

Ronnie made it to the hospital but died a few days later. My mother always believed he had veered into the other lane on purpose. What a horrible thought. If that were true, did he consider how his actions would affect all the others involved in the crash or on the road that day? What about his family? Was he really that self-absorbed and troubled? I'm afraid the answer is probably yes.

Two disturbing things happened after Ronnie's death. The first was an oddly written obituary describing him only as the "son of Ralph R. Tanner, an employee of the city of Port Lavaca" with no mention of his mother.

Even more crushing for my grandmother was when Paw-Paw stormed through the house, taking down every last photo or memento of Ronnie's life and accomplishments, throwing them in a box, and issuing the edict that he never wanted to hear his son's name again. It was as if in their home, Ronald Tanner had never existed. This was my grandfather's way of grieving.

So Maw-Maw kept that little box of memories buried on a high shelf in her closet. Every now and then, she would secretly take it down and indulge her primal need to remember her only son. She finally entrusted the box to me in hopes that if she died before Paw-Paw, Ronnie's name wouldn't be completely extinguished.

The combination of suffocating grief and Paw-Paw's increasing anger caused Maw-Maw to cling even more tightly to her savior. She had nowhere else to turn.

The crown jewel of Maw-Maw's yellow scrapbook is a heartrending handwritten note detailing a dream she had where Ronnie had appeared to her:

I said, "Ronnie, you know you are dead, don't you?"

He said, "Yes, I know I am dead."
"And you know you have to go back again."
"Yes, I know," he said.
"Are you at peace, Ronnie?"
"Yes, I'm at peace," he said.
"Do you see Jesus?"
"Yes, I see Jesus when I think on him."
This dream I pray the Lord gave me. I've prayed for peace for so long. His will be done. —Lillie

On November 7, 2007, Maw-Maw drew her last breath and was immediately ushered into the arms of Jesus. My mother wrote a lovely obituary tribute, and I wonder if she even realized at the time how her own life longings were reflected in her mother's path: "Had she the opportunity of higher education, she would have excelled in whatever career she chose. Articulate, intelligent, practical, witty, outspoken, and sometimes a tad tart in her remarks…"

She included an eerie foreshadowing of the tragedy of her own final days as she described her mother, who "remained fiercely independent with a sharp mind and excellent memory."

Oddly enough, although my mother did not share Maw-Maw's religious beliefs, she believed those convictions were important enough for a whole paragraph in the obituary. It was as if she understood faith in principle but had decided it wasn't for her. She wrote this about her mother:

> *She was, above all, the strongest of believers in God and the risen Christ. Her faith was all-encompassing, high, wide, and deep, and though tested by many sorrows, she remained a true disciple in word and action.*

When someone you love so very much passes away, it can be heartbreaking, but knowing Maw-Maw was in the presence of the God she loved so much provided immeasurable comfort to me.

But my mother was not so convinced she would ever see Maw-Maw again.

CHAPTER 2
Gloria

The fifties—they seem to have taken place on a sunny afternoon that asked nothing of you except a drifting belief in the moment and its power to satisfy.

—Elizabeth Hardwick, "Domestic Manners"

AS DIFFICULT AS my mom's early life was, I have to believe she found some joy in those hope-filled teen years of the 1950s teeming with possibilities. The world moved quickly those days, with the threat of war gone and the economic fuel of conflict providing a comfortable life for families like the Tanners. Elvis was king, and the shadow of nuclear war between superpowers was yet an indistinct smudge on the horizon. The small town of Port Lavaca cradled its citizens in bustling optimism. Outside the four walls of Mother's home, life was good. A far cry from the

Cunningham's idyllic existence in *Happy Days*, I know, but surely she had moments of satisfaction and glimpses of self-worth courtesy of her many achievements.

Gloria Tanner's excellence mindset continued to reward her with high marks at school and in her extracurricular endeavors. I can picture her holed up in her room in the evenings, fighting anxiety at the thought of missing even one point on the next day's exam, typing and retyping essays and research papers until even the most critical eye would not be able to spot an error, struggling to shut out the sounds of her father's latest tirade.

Mother was a planner, a dreamer. She yearned to go to college, but Paw-Paw would not allow it. Even pleading for help establishing a career in "women's vocations," such as nursing or secretarial work, was to no avail. She was forbidden to even apply for scholarships because no one was going to learn Ralph Tanner couldn't afford college for his daughter. Eventually, Mother's academic prowess earned her a full-ride scholarship offer to the University of Texas. I can imagine the blood rushing to her head when she opened that letter, her mind racing with possibilities. Would she study teaching? Or history? Maybe music. She could do anything she wanted!

But, predictably, Paw-Paw had other ideas, patently forbidding her from accepting. No woman needed a college education, he said. That was just foolishness. She cried for weeks as she read and reread that offer. Was Paw-Paw's own inferiority at play, or did the fear she would outshine her little brother prompt him to slam the door of opportunity in her face? My guess is it was just plain messed-up thinking. It seems Paw-Paw struggled with his grip on reality.

It seems odd to me that she didn't simply go against her father's wishes and enroll anyway, but that was not how things worked in their world.

Music was Mother's escape. The halls of Calhoun High School reverberated as her lovely soprano melded with the class of 1960 choir.

By this time, her skill as an organist had earned her a permanent place as a volunteer musician at church each week. She was lauded as a talented singer and instrumentalist, often tapped to accompany others, using her gift of teaching and coaching to bring out their best work. She bitterly recounted the story of her father refusing to allow her to travel to a state choir competition, citing the cost of the requisite ensemble of a simple black skirt and white blouse as too outlandish. She and Maw-Maw offered solution after solution for the expense and effort required to attend the event, but he would not be swayed. When Paw-Paw decided he was right, it was as if black-and-white facts and plain common sense were nowhere to be found. I had firsthand experience with this myself.

Once while we were visiting him after hernia surgery, he began to rail against the surgeons: "I could have gotten a knife and done the surgery better than this damn doctor did."

Lord knows why. Maybe I was just too young to realize the dangerous line I was about to cross, but I tried to reason with him. "Now, Paw-Paw," I said innocently, "why would you even say that? You know that's not true."

"Girl," he shouted, "you don't tell me that! You just need to keep your mouth shut. I know what I'm talking about, and I could do it. I could do it right now!"

I don't have a lot of memories of him focusing his delusional anger on me, but this was one I'll never forget. It takes a hard man to stoop to that level of rage with a child.

To Have and To Hold

As much as my mom fought the confines of her role as a woman of that era, her most momentous move really comes as a surprise. As textbook behavior for a teen in an abusive home, at the age of sixteen, she made the choice to become pregnant. Whether that was a purposeful act or a subconscious one, we'll never know. But it was assuredly a choice. I can only hope she wasn't buying the delusion that getting out from under her father's control would free her from all the stifling limitations blocking her path.

Taking a cue from Maw-Maw, my mom later in life wrote her own manifesto, addressed to me, a combination of whining, apologizing, and explaining away why our mother-daughter journey had been so fraught. Near the end of the eight-thousand-word epistle, she finally recounted a little about the events leading up to my birth.

"I have never felt so lost and alone as I did then," she concluded.

She was, of course, terrified of telling her parents she had become pregnant. She assumed Paw-Paw would either "beat her to death" or send her to "one of the homes where you give birth and the baby is taken away." I am grateful she wanted to keep me. In those days, neither abortion nor single parenting were in vogue, so Mother quickly planned to marry my birth father, a fellow high school student.

Monty Tucker was a "decent, nice man," she would later tell me, and she felt fortunate he had taken responsibility for his actions. Although it was the last thing my mother wanted, Maw-Maw and the aunties got busy planning a big church wedding. Donning a white dress and pasted-on smile, Miss Gloria Tanner became Mrs. Monty Tucker.

One classic teen pregnancy scenario my mom refused to give in to was dropping out of high school. After getting married, she created a "major uproar" with the school board by requesting permission to earn her diploma while pregnant. These days, it's hard to imagine that such an obstacle could even exist for a young woman wanting to complete her education. Thankfully, one sympathetic board member cast the vote that allowed her to return. She dug even further into her studies, compacting, with excellence, the next two years' worth of work into one. In so doing, she became the valedictorian of the class of 1959, alongside one of her male cousins, Paw-Paw's brother's son, as salutatorian. She must have felt tremendous satisfaction earning the top spot of the record 118 graduating seniors and securing a place of honor that even her misogynistic father couldn't deny her. The photo from the newspaper clipping tells the story: "Mrs. Tucker" grinning proudly through what I assume was perfect red lipstick. It must have been a moment of real pride for the whole family. For years, Mother was haunted by a dream where she stood at the door of the high school, yearning to join her classmates in their senior year, but no one would let her in. She would wake to a pillow wet with tears.

Halfway through that stressful final year of school, she gave birth to a little girl and named her Allison. She loved that I was a girl, not a boy.

My mom was, not surprisingly, unhappy in her first marriage, which had started with the odds stacked precipitously against it. She was, after all, still a child herself, struggling to fit the mold of the '50s housewife when her friends were going to prom. Grieving lost opportunities to find her own way in the world. Dealing with one of those little smelly babies she so disliked. She eventually had to take a part-time job, which was probably a relief because that meant she could shuttle me off to Maw-Maw for care and keeping. This was where my spiritual and emotional foundation was poured. Where Maw-Maw taught me to pray and taught me to love.

Mother taught me it's possible to live in perpetual melancholy, blaming others for the hand she was dealt. Blaming herself for derailing her life before it even started.

She insisted none of her unhappiness was my fault, but we both knew that wasn't true. From the moment I was born, a barrier existed between us. One that, in the end, harmed her much more than it harmed me.

Dad

My birth certificate lists Monty Tucker as my father, but by the time of my first memories, they had divorced, and Mother had married the man I called Dad, Lyman Saylor. At one point, he officially adopted me, and my last name changed from Tucker to Saylor. The implications of that were lost on me at that young age. I had never known Monty Tucker, although my grandmother recalled him coming to visit a few times after the divorce, bringing me pretty little dresses, until Mother cut him off. She never explained that choice, and I never asked for one.

Dad was an older man, an exciting, intelligent, well-traveled World War II veteran who attracted Mom with the depth and breadth of exotic life experience. He taught her to drive and shared her love of gardening and cats. He met her intensity with his own, and, truth be told, his controlling tendencies surely reminded her of her own father. The psychologists would have had a heyday with this.

They had both been married when they met, and both divorced shortly thereafter. He had three other children and was not interested in starting over, which was just fine with my mom. She hated kids. In fact, Dad said she was the most nonmaternal woman he had ever met. There was no chance I would ever be a big sister.

Lyman's parents, who insisted I call them Grandmother and Grandfather Saylor, lived in Goldthwaite, in central Texas, a day's drive from Port Lavaca, his ex and my three stepsiblings just down the road from them. We would visit at Thanksgiving, filling frosty buckets with pecans from their orchard, playing hide-and-seek with my sister and brothers, posing as one happy family.

Even at my young age, I could sense the tension between Grandmother Saylor and my mom. Things were always just a bit awkward and cold. I wonder now if my mom had been looked at as "the other woman" since they married so soon after his divorce. Mother later wrote that Dad often had a hard time meeting child support payments and had to ask his parents to step in. As in any divorce situation, the circumstances were not ideal.

Mother went out of her way to win Grandmother Saylor's approval. At Thanksgiving, she would present Grandmother with a "Twelve Days of Christmas" box filled with homemade trinkets to be opened as the season unfolded. Lavender sachets made from our garden's bounty, crochet-trimmed hand towels, cross-stitched pillowcases, and any number of wrapped gifts spilled from the box. Mother made more of an attempt to engage with her husband's parents than I'd ever seen her do with anyone else, but no matter what she tried, the distance between them would not close.

A few times, Grandmother Saylor came to stay with us in Port Lavaca. She was what we would call today old-school and remained prim and proper at all times. She was, honestly, a pretty imposing presence in my little-girl mind. She would give us a warning if it was to be our turn to say the blessing before a meal, and I would sweat as I worked out just the right words in my head before that performance was called upon. I remember holding my breath as one of the cats in the house—we always had cats in the house—decided to pounce on her perfectly coiffed hairdo before bolting under the couch. Nothing so raucous would have occurred in her home.

She was not, however, a real influence on me because she did not allow herself to be.

Making a Home

Everything my mom did, she did to perfection. She crocheted and taught me to crochet. She learned counted cross-stitch and taught me the same. Every time I return to Port Lavaca, I run across someone who tells me they have something she made for them: doilies, crocheted snowflakes and Christmas trees, personalized wall hangings. She bought me my first sewing machine and helped me, sometimes pretty impatiently, figure out how to use it. I still remember the first article of clothing I made—an orange-and-white gingham nightgown trimmed with orange rickrack. Iconic '60s' stuff. She made me tear out the hem and redo it because it was not straight enough. That infuriated me but was no surprise, as her mantra was "If it's worth doing, it's worth doing right."

Music was a point of connection for Mom and me. We played duets with our four wooden recorders (flutophones)—soprano, alto, tenor, and bass. Sometimes, we would even perform together at church. She was a hard taskmaster with a flawless musical ear. She expected perfection from her students as well. I labored to be perfect myself because, although she never said she loved me, when I met or exceeded her expectations, she would say she was proud of me. That was a balm I didn't even realize at the time my soul needed.

A beautiful grand piano took pride of place in our living room, hymns and classical music echoing from our walls, especially on Saturdays. She attempted to teach me to play, which neither of us particularly enjoyed, and we soon gave that up. I did find a measure of success with the French horn, Mother as my accompanist, making all-state band my senior year. It was a rare point of connection that still holds a special spot in my memories. My friends would request that Mother accompany them to University Interscholastic League performances and competitions because she didn't just play along—she would coach them. *No, this is the crescendo. Try again with more pianoforte.* She brought a passion that rubbed off on those under her tutelage.

Teaching was something that Mother always gravitated toward. Saturdays, in addition to hymns on the piano, she would spread Sunday school materials out on the table to prepare for the next day's lesson. She served each summer during Vacation Bible School. I loved those long, hot mornings at church, pledging allegiance to flags and the

Bible, gulping Kool-Aid out of little Dixie cups, and rejoicing when the craft of the day involved glitter. If Mother could have earned her way to heaven by working for the church, she would have been a VIP.

Although she did not have a teaching degree, when I got into junior high, my mom began working as a substitute, the start of an eighteen-year career in education. She loved it, and students loved her. She would often receive requests from teachers going out on maternity leave because Mother earned a reputation as being more than a classroom babysitter. When she entered the scene, she required excellence and progress. To this day, I have people tell me she was the best teacher they ever had.

Mother's childhood at the home place had seared a deep love of the outdoors into her spirit. She loved to garden and spent countless hours digging in the dirt, caring for flowers, trees, and shrubs. When I was little, Dad built her a greenhouse attached to our external garage. This was her sanctuary. She started every plant from seed, diligently replanting them into bigger and bigger pots until the threat of frost had passed.

Mother made a little space in the greenhouse flower bed for me, and she began teaching me how to choose, sow, weed, and harvest my own crop of veggies and flowers. The long Texas growing season meant we ate well most months of the year.

In the winter, Mother would reconnoiter, plotting and planning for spring planting. Stacks of colorful books and magazines covered every flat surface of our home as she diagrammed flower beds, sketched designs, and scribbled shopping lists. It was a red-letter day when the seed catalogs began landing in the mailbox.

Mother would cycle through phases and fads in landscaping, including one period featuring a tailored English gardening style. Carefully sculpted hedges framed ivy-covered fences and provided a beautiful backdrop to the delicate lavender bushes. She dragged urns and stepping stones through the yard until things looked like they were ready for a magazine shoot. She had me on hands and knees trimming grass from around tree trunks to complete the picture of flawlessness. Anyone who saw the garden at the end of her life, a purposefully natural habitat for all things wild, would not have believed such a highly manicured yard had ever been her choice.

I treasured our hours in the garden together. When my mother and I were working side by side, sweat dripping in our eyes, sharing the satisfaction of creating something beautiful, the connection was undeniable. We were a family.

Theirs was not an epic love story, but my memories of growing up were not of constant tension and outbursts. My mom's thoughts always tended toward the negative, and in the end, she disputed my rosy recollections. Of course, she had the perspective of the one who had to make sure there was enough food in the house and the electric bill was paid. She lamented the fact that for the first couple years of their marriage, Dad did not even allow her access to their checking account.

I wish I could have given Mother my positive perspective on my childhood. In my mind, things were happy, and we were content. I see now that my dad had a cruel streak that he leveraged against both my mom and me, the ethos of the time granting permission for the man of the house to do as he wished. We would deal with that in God's time.

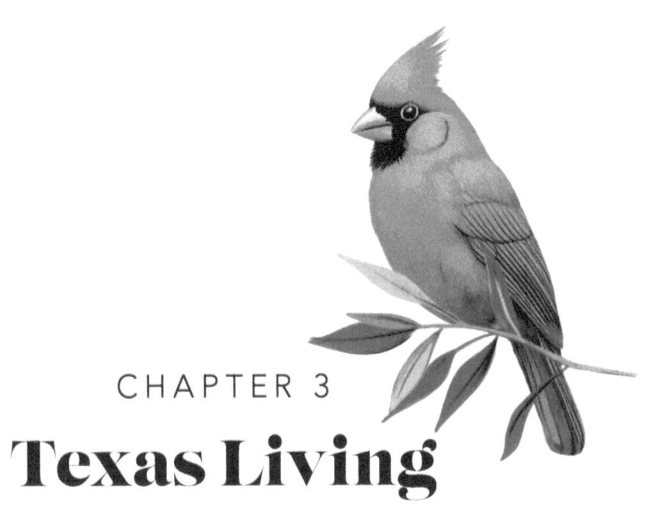

CHAPTER 3
Texas Living

We can sometimes love what we do not understand, but it is impossible completely to understand what we do not love.

—Anna Brownell Jameson

I'VE HEARD IT said that when someone dies, a library burns to the ground. Every memory, every piece of knowledge amassed, every nugget of wisdom earned, becomes inaccessible to those who remain. Oh, how I wish I had gathered more of those treasures from my parents and grandparents when I could, tucking away advice and comfort to be consulted as struggles arise. How did I go all those years without asking simple questions? *What was it like when you were twelve, Mom? Have you ever been afraid? What is your best memory of me?*

How I would love to hear my mother talk about the days when I was growing up, skipping off to school with homework tucked neatly in my backpack and a healthy lunch in the brown paper sack I was to use multiple times. *Waste not; want not.* What did she do all day when I was gone? Did she look forward to my return at three o'clock or dread the interruption I caused to her personal agenda? Had she ever truly loved my dad, or had theirs been an impulsive marriage of convenience—financial support for her and a housekeeper for him?

These people I loved and continue to love so desperately, those souls that made my existence possible, are simply no longer here. Other than that handful of heartfelt and often brutal letters left behind in dusty boxes, their counsel is no longer available to help me navigate the next step on my path. To help make sense of the very grown-up things that went on all around me when I was young.

Shadows of the Past

Linda, my childhood best friend, lived just down the street. Hers was a home full of noise and love. With six kids in the house, it was an adventure for me to visit, observing the large Catholic family dynamics and soaking in the chaos. But it was there I realized I was a bit of an introvert, frequently needing to flee the constant stimulation and retreat to my quiet house, snuggling cats in my lap, listening to Mother's sewing machine hum.

My parents and I didn't take traditional family vacations, which was another one of those things that I didn't know I was missing because I didn't have a normal frame of reference. One reason for our lack of travels, I'm sure, was a shortage of funds. I have to wonder if they also hesitated to take elaborate trips with me because my dad felt it wasn't fair to his other children. Mom and Dad loved history, but they hated crowds, so when school started in the fall, they would take off to explore Civil War battlefields and other historical sights, leaving me in Maw-Maw's care. Yet whenever a school trip came up, Mother made sure the funds were there. She would never say no to something like that.

Both of my parents worked hard, Dad performing many of our home repairs and updates. I didn't pay much attention to things like how much money we had, but Mother told me later they were always struggling, especially since he had another household to support. I remember the *click-click* of the little plastic handheld device Mother would use to tally groceries as we loaded the cart—one click per cent, one per dime, or one per dollar. There was no credit card to fall back on or option to go over the predetermined total by even one penny; Daddy gave her twenty dollars a week for food, and there was zero wiggle room. I never even bothered asking for a treat. She talked about Daddy gambling to make the ninety-one-dollar house payment each month. I remember a giant television cable spool we pulled from the trash and repurposed as a side table. We refinished secondhand furniture and sewed our own table covers and curtains. All the handmade gifts my mom crafted, in hindsight, were her solution to stay within budget constraints. She remembered only one good year, 1963, when money wasn't a worry.

For many years, Daddy's pride wouldn't allow Mom to take a job, but he finally succumbed to her wish to substitute teach. She later told me that Dad used the term "allow her to work," a phrase that rankled her until the day she died. She was "allowed," that is, as long as she came home to put his lunch on the table every day. Why the men of that generation insisted upon having women put their food on the table has always puzzled me, but that was how they operated.

Although I didn't realize it at the time, one of the oddest turning points between my mother and me was her insistence that I pursue a college degree. And not just any college degree—a BS in chemical engineering from Texas A&M University. As all teenagers do, I dreamed of many adult paths, such as taking a gap year to consider my options, traveling, or studying any number of intriguing subjects. We had made it through most of the 1970s, and women could do anything. But math and science came easy to me, so her declaration that I join a well-paying profession was hard to argue against. I certainly had the personality for a detail-oriented career such as engineering. And, she was paying for it, after all, working hard and saving religiously. I once applied for a job at Dairy Queen, and when she found out about it, Mother forced me to withdraw the application. She wanted me to be able to concentrate solely on my studies. Dad would not contribute to my college because he could not afford to do so for his other three children as well. Rebelling against Mother's prescriptive plan did not seem like a good idea. In fact, I can't remember even considering telling her no. I don't even remember thinking about doing it. That's just not how the dynamics of our house worked. The strange thing was how she was blind to the fact that her controlling insistence was not that different from that of her own father. The same suffocating force that had derailed her educational hopes and dreams was being leveraged against me, and this time, she was the bully. I couldn't see it at the time either.

Off to College Station

The premier choice for chemical engineering in Texas was Texas A&M University, so that's the only school I applied to. When the day came to pack up the car and head up the highway the three hours to College Station, I don't know who was more excited, Mother or me. There was not a coed-parent team arriving on campus that day that was better prepared than we were. Mom had spent weeks mending and updating my wardrobe. She pored over catalogs and book lists with me, making sure I had everything I needed and a few luxuries besides. She checked and double-checked my boxes, counted and recounted my spending money, and was more positive and upbeat than I had seen her since we found our missing cat holed up in a box in the garage.

She said she was proud of me.

Those were the days before texting and emails, before instant messaging or even voicemail. If you wanted to communicate with someone, you either did it in person, over a landline phone call, or through a letter. Being on my own to that extent was both exhilarating and horrifying. In hindsight, I realize my decision-making skills were not what they should have been at that point simply because I hadn't voiced many of my own choices over the years. When Mother weighed in on a situation, that was that.

But she also wasn't someone I would consult when I needed advice because if I chose a solution different than the one she put forth, she would react in anger and stack yet another brick in the wall between us. Mother wasn't the kind of person you could just sit down with and engage in small talk about your day or life in general. "Shooting the breeze" was not in her vocabulary. She was very practical and guarded, especially when the long-distance phone charges were top of mind. She often reprimanded me for racking up the phone bill, which really hurt because it was my lifeline to home during those first semesters away. Our stilted phone calls would go like this:

Mother: Hello, Allison. I'm going to come for the day on Saturday. I got those curtains done for your room and mended your purple sweater. Do you need anything else?

Me: No, thank you, Mom.

Mother: All right, I will see you around noon.

Me: Sounds good. See you then.

Click.

That would be it. All business, no chatting, no emotion.

I would overhear the other girls on the phone with their moms and even their dads, answering question after question about campus life, drinking in updates about what was going on at home, crying and laughing as they connected with their parents. The strangest part? They would almost always end the calls by saying, "I love you too."

I love you too. Four words I had never said to my mom because it would have necessitated her saying, "I love you" first.

Mother loved my college suitemates and would always bring along handmade gifts for them, crocheted doilies or cross-stitched linens. She made day trips often during my college years, drinking in the sights and sounds of the halls of learning. We logged hours walking through the library, the brick buildings that housed my classrooms, and even the wide-open fields of campus. We would grab lunch and do some window shopping, never purchasing clothes, of course, because she could recreate them herself. Mother would stock up on supplies at her favorite needlework shop. She seemed to revel in those visits, her green eyes lighting up whenever I complained about a professor or griped about a cafeteria meal. Although the things I was learning in math and science classes were lost on her, she was a great help with my English classes, always willing to employ her red pen to boost my grade.

Mother would occasionally comment about how she never got to experience these university rites of passage that I took for granted, but I wasn't in tune enough at the time to realize what she was really doing there. Why she made it a priority to spend six hours in the car and one of her two precious weekend days coming to see me. I guess I desperately needed to believe she was starting to tear down those barriers of disapproval and aloofness that defined our relationship. That was part of it, but she later wrote, "I lived the college life vicariously through you; they were the best years of my life with you… I essentially went back to high school with you and then saw what college was like; it was grand. I know I made a pest of myself, coming up all the time, but it was such a dream that you were getting what I missed."

I don't remember her being a pest. Those years were also a highlight for me, stitching together hours of mostly peaceful companionship.

My first couple semesters as an Aggie slipped into a familiar rhythm of cracking open books, building friendships, and entertaining my mom. I felt keenly the pressure of being in the female minority in the engineering college, along with the ubiquitous expectation to excel that my mother placed upon me. As an upperclassman, I began working for Union Carbide on school breaks, helping offset some of my educational costs. From that point on, between heavier class content and work hours, I became too busy to entertain her as much. The visits dwindled.

Most of the family I had left behind in Port Lavaca continued to attend church, some drawing closer to Christ and some mired in the sludge of unworthiness. Maw-Maw would write often, detailing her daily chores, what the aunties were up to, what was sprouting in the garden, what they were canning, naturally slipping in the ways God was working in her life. Once, during those early weeks away from home, she signed a letter, "Love, Grandma." The next time I was home, I confronted her about it, and she sheepishly said she thought Maw-Maw was a title she should outgrow to save me from embarrassment. I let her know she would be Maw-Maw until the very end. And she was.

Maw-Maw would gently ask if I was going to church each week, as if she could gauge by my habits if I was on the right path. She told me she prayed for me every day, and I believed her. The background noise of her love fueled my success.

When I graduated, the distance between Mother and me widened even further. I think any parent struggles with how to let go as their responsibility wanes, the *I've-got-you-raised-and-now-you-need-to-make-it-on-your-own* attitude. You don't expect them to just walk away, to take on the viewpoint that they are done with you. But that's how she handled it. It was as if she flipped the Mom switch to the off position and moved on to other things. I know now that it was just a symptom of the complicated ball of dysfunction she called life, but it still hurt.

She became a vegetarian. And, God love her, she became a stereotypical, albeit organized, cat lady.

That was when I learned the meaning of the word *ornithology*. Freed from the burden of tuition payments, Mother put down deposits on vacations to exotic locales such as the Fiji Islands. In place of college visits, she boarded planes with her camera and bird-watching companions. She wrote of "struggling up the Andes in Peru and almost getting altitude sickness but managing to see that beautiful diademed sandpiper-plover bathing in the rivers of the Amazon." She was able to pet a baby kangaroo in Papua New Guinea, ride camels and elephants in Asia, and go birding in Argentina with the renowned Phoebe Snetsinger, "the greatest and nicest birder who ever lived." Mother even told the story of narrowly avoiding being bitten by a venomous Western diamondback in the mountains of West Texas, saved by her providential purchase of rattlesnake boots from J. C. Melcher's hardware store in Port Lavaca.

Trekking all over the world, she would spend an inordinate amount of time and money, in my view, just to see a bird or experience a rush of adrenaline. She invited me on a couple of local excursions, but it just never took with me. The phone calls petered out, and things between us became very distant. And what could I do? I was busy working full-time and planning my own future. I told myself I didn't need her either.

As our extended family began to spread out and age, Mother spent less and less time with most of them as well. She did keep in touch with one of her cousins, Melvin, who was also my godfather. She loved to make the two-hour drive to Houston to spend the day with him, lunching at a little bistro or strolling through nurseries for landscape and garden ideas. I think it was an escape for her—an excuse to get out of the house and away from my dad. When she began to pull ever further away from me, I turned to Melvin for advice and comfort; he knew her background better than anyone and didn't try to make excuses.

"I don't know why she's that way," he would say with heartfelt sympathy. "It just breaks my heart." However, we both knew that if he had chastised or criticized her, she would have shut him down as well. Mother did not like to be second-guessed or told she was doing something wrong, and if you delivered a message like that, there would be no forgiveness. No second chances. Those who were close to her, like Melvin or even her church friends, knew the boundaries and limits of what they could say and were not willing to poke the bear. The walls stood high and wide.

Adulting

When I graduated from Texas A&M in the early 1980s, the economy was not strong, especially as it related to the oil business. I received one job offer that would have taken me back to Port Lavaca, but as I was considering the ramifications of that move, another opportunity arose at Halliburton Field Service in North Texas, an eight-hour drive from home. I was used to being the odd woman out in my engineering classes, but no one ever had the nerve to tell me I didn't belong. Yet once some of those good old boys found out I had been offered a field position in the oil industry, they couldn't hold back their opinions. One even had the audacity to tell me "women don't work in the oil field." Indeed, they did not. But I was hard-headed enough to pave the way. That was the beginning of what Mother called my "horrendously busy" adult life, and indeed, my job was extremely demanding, always requiring more than a forty-hour workweek. But she was still proud of me.

Mother and I took one vacation together to Yellowstone and the Grand Tetons during the early days of my career, in search of birds and common ground.

After a couple years working as a field service engineer, a dashing younger man joined our team. For a time, I was actually his supervisor, and when we began to date, we anticipated some fallout. Romantic relationships on the job were a very new concept in this male-dominated business, and we weren't sure what to expect. One day, the yard boss confronted me.

"Hey, I heard you and Doug might be going out," he said, tiptoeing into the unfamiliar waters.

"Yeah, we might be."

"Well, we really can't have that. You're going to have to quit seeing him, or one of y'all's going to have to quit."

"OK, I'll quit," I quipped.

Well, he wasn't expecting that. In true Saylor fashion, I called his bluff, and he lost the more experienced employee. I knew it would be easier to find another good job than it would be to find another good man.

Although I suspected the mother-daughter relationship I had grown up with was odd, nothing exposed the dysfunction more than the day I met Doug's parents. You see, they were huggers. In fact, I have often said they were the "huggingest" people I had ever met. Hug when you arrive, hug when you have good news, hug when you have bad news, and, of course, a *big* hug on your way out the door. They even said, "I love you." Out loud. *These people are strange*, I thought.

After a season of courtship, Doug and I became engaged. Doug likes to say he couldn't work for me, so he decided to marry me instead.

Mother had no input on wedding decisions because she thought the whole thing was a bad idea. She was less than supportive—she was demoralizing. In her mind, marriage was the great enemy that stopped forward progress and slammed prison bars shut on women.

"Getting married is going to ruin your career," she said more than once. I had to remind her that it was no longer the 1950s. Helen Reddy had long since belted out her anthem, and women were indeed roaring in numbers too big to ignore. But I knew my decision to dismiss her directive would have a consequence. Another brick went up, another layer for the veil of isolation she wore with aplomb.

Rather than my wonderfully talented mother sewing my wedding dress, I did it myself. But in a strange twist that came to light as I was going through her things recently, Doug found a little black and white photo of my mother's first wedding, the one to my biological father, and her dress was strikingly similar to mine. Go figure.

Whatever Mother's objections to my marriage, I think she carried the classic notion that no man was good enough for her little girl. She would not have been supportive of me marrying anyone, but she focused her ire on Doug, setting the stage for their less-than-ideal relationship that would unfold over the coming decades. Please understand that from where I stood, Doug, for the most part, remained the picture of grace, but her coldness toward him created a perfectly stereotypic mother-in-law situation.

One time, I asked her why she didn't like Doug. She said, "Because he's too hard-headed and opinionated."

Pot, meet the kettle, I thought. Then I said it out loud. That did not go over well.

A Tale of Two Religions

Doug and I exchanged vows in our local Lutheran church on a sticky fall day in 1985. Our early married life included Sunday visits to my in-laws, attending their Baptist services, and enjoying a meal together. Those times were such amazing learning opportunities for me, and I marveled at the easygoing exchange of love and affection that went on in their home. Doug's mom, Ellen, nurtured me in ways I hadn't even realized I needed. We had those long, intimate parental phone calls I had eavesdropped on in college. She cared about me and wasn't afraid to say it. At first, it was strange to be asked—without judgment or agenda—about my feelings or my motivations for doing the things I did. But eventually, her open arms and open heart became my safe space. A space padded with understanding and forgiveness.

Unlike my parents, grandparents, and great-grandparents, who had stayed married not out of love but because they felt trapped, the Crabtrees transferred a legacy of healthy commitment in marriage to me. It was the perfect gift.

On the weekends when Doug and I stayed home, we had fallen out of the habit of church attendance—an easy thing for me to do since it didn't mean much more than keeping up an old family tradition. But Doug, having been raised in a home where authentic relationships with Christ were cultivated, was missing that connection. One day, as I was sitting in the little front room of our first house, sewing, and thinking, Doug walked in and casually suggested we attend the revival going on at our local Baptist church. I hesitated, and in hindsight, I know there was a definite spiritual tug-of-war playing out in that room, but after due consideration, I agreed to go.

If you ever attended a Southern Baptist revival in the 1980s, you can picture the scene: spirit-filled four-part hymn singing and a knockout message reminiscent of the "Sinners in the Hands of an Angry God" sermon. I don't remember the closing song, the invitation to walk up to the altar and profess faith in Christ, but it was likely the Baptist revival anthem "Just as I Am":

> Just as I am and waiting not
> To rid my soul of one dark blot;
> To Thee whose blood can cleanse each spot,
> Oh Lamb of God, I come, I come!

I felt such a strong pull to repent and ask Christ to cover my sins—every wrong thought and action—with his sacrifice. I stood to go forward and pray with the pastor. Poor Doug, thinking he had pressured his little mainline Lutheran bride into doing something rash, reached up to stop me.

But there was no stopping me.

When we told his parents about what evangelicals call my "confession of faith," they were thrilled and shared that they had prayed I would enter into a real relationship with God through Christ. I wrote to Maw-Maw, and she was just so happy. It was at that point she and I entered a period of deep fellowship with each other. I had so much to learn. I knew the Bible stories and tenets of the church, but how did that play out in daily life? How could I really know what the Lord's plan was for me? And how could I convince Mom she needed a savior?

CHAPTER 4
Twilight Gathers

Beware of parting! The true sadness is not in the pain of the parting: it is in the when and how you are to meet again with the face about to vanish from your view.

—*Edward Bulwer-Lytton*

AFTER FIFTEEN YEARS in the school system, Mother began dreading those sunrise phone calls requesting she cover for a teacher who would be out. Because of her disdain for young children, she always opted for middle or high school classes, where educators were becoming more and more often called upon to be disciplinarians. She carried increased tension as she entered a classroom, wondering what conflicts would distract from the learning she had planned. It was barely worth the fifteen dollars a day the substitutes brought home. When the weight of her responsibilities eventually tipped from being more crisis control than teaching, she was done.

Mother took a job at a real estate office making $3.50 an hour, a substantial pay raise, especially since the hours were regular and not based on the fluctuating needs of the school system. Unfortunately, the money came with an equally impressive load of work. For the next twenty-four years, she juggled the odd hours of the real estate sales profession, covering the phone at the office during business hours and taking calls on evenings, weekends, and holidays. Even when Paw-Paw was dying of liver cancer, she had to keep up with her tasks, often returning to the office after taking Maw-Maw to visit him in the hospital each evening. Mother "did the work of three people" and, I'm sure, put her drive for excellence on display every day.

During these years, she also realized her lifelong dream of being a college co-ed, taking night classes at the University of Houston-Victoria, but never graduated. I'm sure she was a straight-A student.

Although my memories of Daddy when Doug and I would visit were that he was a much better host than Mother was hostess, she told me later that the visits caused him inordinate stress. I think that was her way of letting me know they caused her inordinate stress. Both Mother's and my relationship with Dad had been complicated, but at the point my marriage began, theirs was all but over. Doug and I did not go to Port Lavaca often, and my mother's aloofness had not abated, so the subtleties of the situation were lost on me. Later, Mother wrote that she had been physically afraid of Dad, yet more afraid of her perceived inability to make a living. She escaped into birding, he into drinking and skiing with a group of friends. "Our lives were totally separate for the last twenty-five years," she said. They remained married in name only.

Daddy loved to take long ski trips with his buddies, frequenting the slopes of Red River, New Mexico, Park City, Utah, and even some in Canada. Their favorite time of year was January after the Christmas skiers had vacated the slopes while there was still fresh powder to be conquered. It was on one of these vacations that Dad's friends noticed he had taken on an almost-zombie-like countenance. He had long suffered from back pain and been a champion self-medicator, maintaining a close relationship with the local pharmacist. I assume he was mixing alcohol with those pain pills on that trip and things just went too far. His friends contacted Mother about their concerns, and she eventually took him to the doctor, where the source of his back pain was finally diagnosed: bone cancer. And it was bad.

On the Texas Gulf Coast, there is at least a perception that there's an increased risk of developing unattributable cancer and other maladies. Someone who had never smoked would get lung cancer. Someone without sun-damaged skin would develop melanoma. When my Paw-Paw, who didn't drink, ended up with liver cancer, I remember saying, "Well, that's strange."

Mother replied, "No, it's not strange. You've got all these damn petrochemical plants down here."

When I suggested that, in that case, maybe she should move, she said, "It's too late. We're going to get it. We're going to die." That was not only illustrative of her defeatist attitude but also a shadow of things to come.

Foxholes and Deathbeds

They say there are no atheists in foxholes or on deathbeds. Daddy, who had spent plenty of time in foxholes, had consistently proclaimed "religion" to be a crutch for people to lean on. I don't know that he was truly an atheist, but I do know he did not believe in a creator God or a need for a savior. Ashes to ashes, dust to dust. End of story. I had talked to him about his need for the Lord and prayed regularly for him, but when the cancer diagnosis was announced, my prayers gained a new fervency: *God, please open the door and give me the willingness to step through and follow your will.* I knew I couldn't do it on my own.

The stubborn, eccentric war veteran had always been under the illusion that he was in control of his life. Unfortunately, that frame of mind translated into taking steps to ensure he never had to suffer the indignities that come with end-stage disease. So, a few weeks before he succumbed to that horrid cancer, he tried to take his own life. In God's perfect plan, a praying friend of his happened to heed the call of his spirit to knock on Daddy's door that day. When no one answered, the man looked in the window, saw what Daddy was doing, and intervened by breaking the window. Daddy was very angry that his efforts had been thwarted, but I was so grateful to have more time. Such a concrete reminder that God is in control and to take every prompting of the Holy Spirit seriously.

Not long after that incident, I went to visit my dad. It had only been a few months since the diagnosis, but the medication and disease had already robbed him of the ability to even know I was there. I prayed out loud and didn't even know if he heard it, but God did. It was with a heavy heart that I left him that weekend. Dealing with the death of one so close is something we will all face. But when you are sure they have chosen to spend eternity in hell, the burden is unbearable. I felt like God had let me down. Was there really no hope?

On my final visit, I held his hand, stroked his cheek, and yearned to see signs that he recognized my presence. For two days, there were none. The day I was to fly home was one of the hardest of my life. Having to say goodbye to someone you know you'll not see again in this life is an excruciating thought. I almost didn't take the two-block walk from Mother's house to the hospital.

But I'm glad I did.

I cautiously entered that hospital room, honestly not knowing if he was dead or alive, much less if he was lucid. The beeping monitors ensured me he was still with us. The shades were drawn, and his life was slipping away.

"Hi, Daddy, it's Allison," I said. And he ever so slowly turned his head toward my voice. He knew I was there! And, more importantly, I knew God was there.

His hands were cold. So cold. But I held them as I wiped his eyes and smoothed back his hair. Then God gave me the sermon of a lifetime, and I delivered the words. I hate to think what someone would have thought if they had come through the door in those following minutes because I was not mincing words. I was pretty stern.

> *Daddy, I love you. I am so sorry you are having to go through this, but you and I have to talk. All your life, you have turned your back on religion and said it was just a crutch, but it's not. It's real. You are one of the smartest men I've ever known. It's time to quit being stubborn and make the right decision. Daddy, you don't have much time left on this earth. And after today, after I leave this room, I will never see you alive on earth again. I want to see you again when I get to heaven.*
>
> *God is real. And God loves you. To turn your back on God doesn't mean you get to just ignore what comes after you leave this life. To not choose God is to choose to spend an eternity in hell. Daddy, I don't want that for you. I love you.*
>
> *Daddy, listen to me. You don't have to say anything. God knows you can't speak, but you can feel it in your heart and speak it through your mind. God hears you. Admit you are a sinner. We are all sinners. Ask God to forgive your sins, and he will. Not only are they forgiven, they are forgotten. All sins are forgiven, and I forgive you for*

> *all the ways you hurt me, too. It's only because of Christ's love for me that I can forgive you. Daddy, believe that the man called Jesus Christ, the one you have heard about and turned your back on all these years, believe in your heart that he died on the cross for you. It's not too late yet, but if you wait until your last breath is taken, it will be too late then. Ask God to save you.*

I then explained to him about the thief who hung on the cross next to Jesus, the one who confessed his belief in the final moments of his life, securing a place in paradise. I laid my head on Daddy's chest and prayed. And when I raised my head up, a tear rolled down his cheek.

I shall forever hold on to the hope that, at that moment, he finally understood.

Although my parents had been essentially estranged for decades, I think becoming a widow had a profound effect on my mom's mental state. She had taken good care of him during those final months; although compassion was not her forte, duty certainly was. Fortunately, before Daddy died, in order for her to move on, she decided she had to forgive him for all the conscious and unconscious sins he had committed toward her. When I shared that I, too, had forgiven him because I was required to do so by Jesus's commands, she simply couldn't believe it.

Her Babies

Her cats, as much as they became a nuisance for her and everyone who loved her, provided a sort of unconditional comfort she could only accept from a nonsentient being. Once, out of a desperate need for her to understand how much her continued aloofness pained me, I accused her of loving those furry creatures more than she loved me.

She denied it, dismissing my feelings by saying I was comparing apples to oranges. Here's how she explained her almost primal need to be surrounded by them: "When I wake up in the morning in dread of what problems the day will bring, they pat my face, lie down next to me, and my blood pressure drops. I feel I can make it another day because someone, something, depends on me."

We had always had cats around, to the tune of one or two inside cats and a couple others relegated to the great outdoors. Her need to nurture and provide for those critters just continued to grow as the years went on. If she could have earned a place in heaven by loving God's creatures, she would have been well on her way.

I don't know exactly when she got involved with the animal welfare organizations, but I do know it was because of her friend Juaniece. The two of them were quite a pair: Juaniece all dolled up with stylish clothes, hair and makeup just so, and Mother with her frizzy hair pulled back, bare-faced and dressed to work. And, like everything else Mother got involved in, she put forth one-hundred-percent-plus effort.

When she could escape the demands of the real estate office, she volunteered at the local shelter in the evenings and on weekends, sometimes multiple times a day. They must have loved her. She dove into every job possible, from cleaning cages and administering medicine to posting social media reports and updating the website. The sick animals were her special focus, and I would get to hear about this kitten with pink eye and that one with diarrhea. She wrote a long Christmas letter each year detailing facility upgrades, thanking donors, and reminding people of the need for more volunteers. Once she retired, her trips to the shelter occurred multiple times a day, every day of the year. The other volunteers became her touchpoint.

Mother never turned away a stray. At one point, there were so many cats in her house that there was a litter box in every room. It was embarrassing and more than a little worrisome, but I must say, she kept things as immaculate as possible under the circumstances. She was constantly scooping boxes and crawling around on the floor with a wet paper towel, wiping up messes, wearing herself out on behalf of those cats. She even constructed a little room at the back of the garage for the outside cats. If one of "her babies" got hurt or killed, she spiraled into days of depression after burying them in the backyard.

Her birding trips had convinced her that since most of the world slept on mats on the floor, that was good enough for her. So she got rid of all the beds in the house and would pull a little mat out of the closet each night, unroll it, roll it back up the next morning, and tuck it away. For a while after that declaration, when I would visit, she had a little cot for me to sleep on. Eventually, I fled to my friend Linda's house. Between the uncomfortable sleeping arrangements and the fact I would be closed in a room with at least one litter box ("I'll clean it," she said.), that was a more comfortable arrangement for me.

Mother's growing compulsion to provide for those cats and basically to live in harmony with nature even prompted a shift in her gardening style. At some point, she moved from the traditional suburban landscaping model to more of a natural habitat for plants and animals. This was a great fit for her as it attracted more birds and cut down on the hours needed to care for the yard. A couple that lived in the house behind her were doing the same. By the time she eventually moved out, the house wasn't even visible from the street.

My Babies

I guess it was foolish of me to think things would change once I got pregnant, but I couldn't help envisioning those little people creating such a draw that Mother would not be able to resist. Doug and I both wanted children. There was no question that was the road we yearned to travel together. But at first, we struggled to conceive. There was nothing physically wrong; we simply had to wait for God's timing.

When that little plus sign came up on the pregnancy test, we were over the moon. So it was especially disheartening when we called my mom. We were just so excited—and relieved, to be honest—and desperately wanted her to share in our joy. But, in true form, the first words out of her mouth were, "What's that going to do to your job? You've ruined your career with this, you know."

Par for the course.

All during the pregnancy, she never passed up an opportunity to make sure I understood how much she disliked children. She had no desire to be spit up on, peed on, or made to comfort a fussy baby ever again. When she would work as a long-term sub for a teacher on maternity leave, she dreaded the day the new mom would bring her baby in for show-and-tell with the class, not because it signaled the end of her work but because they would expect her to hold the newborn. She said she would "hang back and cringe."

"I don't know why I'm that way," she would write later. "Maybe because there was no show of affection at home." *A lack of affection at home didn't make me a bad mother*, I wanted to write in reply.

When our first son, John, was born, unlike the mothers of my friends who came for extended postpartum visits, my mom sent a check. She wanted to be called Abuela, but I resisted that. Grandma was not on the table, so we struck a compromise with the sharp abbreviation of Gran. As our family of three became a family of four and then of five with the births of our sons Paul and Luke, any meaningful connection with their grandmother failed to take root. Preschool graduations, elementary school Grandparents' Days, middle school concerts, and high school dances all took place without any photos of my mother supporting her grandchildren with her presence. She was shocked that I took to motherhood so easily, and I enjoyed showing her how it should be done.

Partially to spite my mother and partially because I loved my job, I continued to work full-time as the boys were growing up. We were blessed with the most wonderful help, Ada, who the boys called Nanny. She was the quintessential English nanny: well-trained, compassionate, yet firm—a perfect fit. We sat enthralled by her tales of the bombings in London during World War II. My pregnancies were notoriously difficult, and Nanny would simply move in and take over if things got rough. She was the glue that held things together during those years. Basketball games? Nanny was there. Church fundraisers? Nanny wrote a check. Graduations? Nanny sat, front row if possible, cheering our boys on.

Even after they grew up, the boys went out of their way to visit her. When she passed away in 2024 at the age of ninety, they all took the day off work, with no prompting from me, to honor her at the funeral.

Rather than experiencing any jealousy that Ada was taking her place as the grandma, Mother loved her. I think it relieved some pressure.

Someone else who took pressure off my mother was my mother-in-law. Mother spoke plainly about my relationship with her: "When Ellen entered your life, you finally had the mother you'd always wanted." Yes, yes, I did. Ellen was the one I could turn to with questions about parenting, marriage, God, and just about any topic you can think of. It was by embracing the open-arms atmosphere of her home that I learned that healthy families are not rare. They are not only possible but worth building and protecting. With thanks to God and his mercy, Doug and my little family continues to grow; two daughters-in-law and five grandchildren have joined our brood, and our home rings with joy.

Not How We Do Things

Mother and I, not being raised in the center of large families, remained blissfully ignorant of how chaos reigned in some larger households. Daddy had experienced it with his three other children, I assume, but he, too, always preferred things quiet and orderly.

The first Christmas I spent with Doug's parents and two brothers was eye-opening and a bit horrifying. When it came time to open gifts, everyone just dug in, tearing bows off packages and wadding wrapping paper into balls prior to shooting them, full-court style, into waiting trash bags. It was noisy and overwhelming. You see, it was my family's tradition to take turns opening packages one at a time, untaping edges and carefully folding up the paper to be used again, closing our eyes and feeling inside the box to guess what the gift was. Calm and orderly. This was Christmas.

After having three boys in four years, Doug and I gave in to the chaos theory. It was just too difficult to try to keep things quiet and under control. It took me a while to embrace it, but now I can't imagine things any other way. Mother attempted a few visits, but she was not able to cope. These were the days before everyone dissected mental conditions like they do today, the days before labels such as OCD, ADHD, and autism, but her revulsion to the disorderliness of our home was more than just a choice of not liking something. She literally could not handle it: "I visited as often as I could, but as the boys grew a bit, the house was chaos. So close together in age, so much noise and screaming. I didn't understand children that age, I guess." The Christmas visit she tried to get us to fold the wrapping paper was a difficult one. It was just not how we did things. I had my own home, my own husband, my own children, and this is the way it was. Rather than alleviating some of her loneliness by embracing the life we were building, she curled up even further into herself. Maybe it was out of her control.

The boys learned there were just some things you didn't mention when Gran was around. Somewhere along the line, she shifted from vegetarian to vegan, explaining she wouldn't eat anything that had a face or could have had a face. She didn't want any animal to have to die for her nutrition. After our experience butchering chickens with Grandpa, I couldn't really blame her. And after hanging around with her bohemian birding friends, it didn't come as a great surprise. The trouble was that my husband and boys loved to hunt. It's the way they spend every fall. It is a big deal for them. That was a problem for her. One Christmas, I bought Doug a spotting scope, and, unfortunately, that was a year Mother had decided to visit for the holidays. She also used a spotting scope for her birding, so I was excited to show it to her, thinking there would be a rare point of connection. Boy, did that backfire! She immediately told me she was not interested in touching anything that was connected to hunting and killing animals. I tried to explain that we also enjoyed looking at animals that were not being hunted, but she would not hear of it. After that incident, we reminded the boys every time they got on the phone to thank her for sending a gift, not to mention they had just been hunting.

For all the difficulties in building and maintaining a connection with my family, Mother did love the boys desperately, writing: "What John has been able to accomplish, how Paul is excelling, how awesome Luke is—they have become more than anyone could hope for. I'm very proud of all of them. I wish they were next door to fix a fence, sit down and talk, one-on-one, really listen to them as individuals, the same with you, but time has slipped away."

Oh, Mom, how I wish that could have been true. You have no idea what you missed.

Dress Rehearsal

As the years progressed and our boys grew, Mother and I drifted further and further apart. It was like a cruel game of whack-a-mole. I would push my head up and point out something I didn't like, somehow with the naive optimism my opinion would change her mind for the first time in our relationship, and she would lash out, widening the rift. If she could make the punishing ten-hour drive to

Big Bend National Park, why couldn't she drive up to see us? If she could fly halfway around the world to see a bird, why couldn't she fly to see her grandkids? The answers were always a litany of pity-party excuses, as far as I could see. As our boys got older, and especially after Maw-Maw and Paw-Paw passed away, my trips to Port Lavaca became less and less frequent, not more than one or two a year. Every trip was a trip of obligation.

Doug and I did have a good chuckle one time when he was in Port Lavaca on business and decided to invite Mother out to dinner. That evening, I sat on pins and needles, wondering what would be added to her latest laundry list of criticisms regarding my choices. But during our next phone call, all my mom could talk about was what a lovely time they had had together. The unspoken message? Maybe I had done all right after all. I took it as a win.

As Doug and my family continued to flourish, so did my career. Mother always enjoyed hearing about what I was doing and where I was traveling. She was still living through me the life she never had the opportunity to enjoy. My infrequent visits were awkward and never lasted more than a couple days. I would work through her to-do list, take her out for a meal or two where she would complain about how much things cost, and grind my teeth, watching her climb around on the floor cleaning up cat messes.

Eventually, the goodbyes became more and more difficult for her. They were the only times I can remember her expressing any kind of strongly positive emotion toward me, crying, hugging, and saying, at long last, that she loved me.

My mom was reaping the consequences of self-imposed isolation, and she was desperately lonely. The cats provided in-the-moment comfort, but she had no close relationships. She had long since stopped going to church and had soundly dismissed the spiritual practices Maw-Maw tried so desperately to instill in her. She had birding friends, neighbors, and shelter coworkers who kept tabs on her but no real emotional connections.

When Doug and I realized our dream of buying four hundred acres of pure Texas bliss, with cattle, dogs, and, yes, even cats, we discussed building a little mother-in-law house on the property in the event my mom would ever need care. It makes me grin to think of how this is something Doug would have agreed to without hesitation while silently praying it would never actually happen.

Mother experienced her share of common health problems that plague the active aged, including two broken foot bones and a bad back brought on by years of lifting landscaping rocks and forty-pound bags of cat litter. Her maladies included worn-out knees, and the day finally arrived when she couldn't stand the pain anymore and asked if I would take some time off work to help her with recovery after a total knee replacement. Before the surgery, Mother gave me both medical and durable powers of attorney, a move that would save countless hours of paperwork in the years to come. She consented to my pleas to finally buy a bed, as the doctor had ruled out sleeping on her floor pallets during recovery, and I agreed to scoop the cat boxes every day. The surgery went well. She had spent a couple days in the hospital, returned home, and we were doing fine together, running to therapy daily and getting along better than I was expecting to.

Of course, that couldn't last.

When I say Mother was eccentric, this is the illustration that will help you understand that's no exaggeration. Keep in mind, at this point, her yard was in the "natural habitat" phase, which, to the casual observer, looked like a neglected, overgrown mess. From the road, you couldn't even see most of the property. I had run to the store to pick up something she needed, and when I pulled into the driveway, she was standing outside the garage in her bra and panties. That's a horrifying enough picture, but then I realized she wasn't using her walker. Of course, I jumped out of the car, mortified that the neighbors might be watching and alarmed that she could have fallen while stumbling around the driveway a week postsurgery without anything to hold on to.

Long story short, she assured me no one could see her, and she walked around her yard in her underwear all the time. She didn't need the damn walker because all it was going to do was make her fall. She didn't need me telling her what to do. She was fine.

I packed my bags that day and drove home.

CHAPTER 5
What Is Happening?

Talk not of comfort—'tis for lighter ills; I will indulge my sorrow and give way; To all the pangs and fury of despair.

—*Joseph Addison*

SO THAT WAS our pattern for many years—me sporadically making the drive to visit, and those trips often ending with an argument. She stayed in her corner, and I in mine. Then in early 2019, I noticed Mother's phone calls increasing in frequency. At first, more and more of our conversations centered around something she had lost, like a favorite gardening tool or her house or car keys. Then she began recounting strange goings on she was experiencing at night, voices both inside the house and out in the yard. *It's probably nothing. Just some bad dreams*, I would tell myself as I struggled to keep things afloat in my own life. The boys were grown, our farm bursting with life and endless chores, and my career was in full bloom.

Surely, this was just a phase Mother would work through.

I've always wondered what my mother's IQ was. She was incredibly intelligent and had an impressive mastery of English. It could be really annoying, but I like to think I inherited a drop of that genius.

My mom was always so excited about my professional accomplishments, asking me to send her my new business cards when I got a promotion so she could show her friends, for example. When I graduated with my MBA from Texas Tech as a "pioneer" in a male-dominated field, she made sure everyone in Port Lavaca heard about it. I once sent her a copy of a technical paper I had labored over with two PhDs for an international conference, expecting high praise for the complex article. What I received was a mercilessly red-lined manuscript noting misplaced modifiers, inverted sentences, and illogical transitions galore! She was a virtuoso in the art of language.

So when Mother started to struggle to find the most basic words in our conversations, simple words and phrases just out of reach, I knew something was not right. She tried to hide it, but I could tell she was having trouble conversing. And once a word or phrase flew beyond her grasp, she would panic, pushing any hope of rebounding out the window. One day, while on the phone with me, she was shooing some workers out the front door. I could hear her struggling to tell them to close the door behind them:

"Sh—sh—shut the—the—" she stammered.

"Door?" I interjected.

It was heartbreaking to hear, and Doug and I began to realize her cognitive abilities were failing fast. We brainstormed what could possibly be causing the precipitous decline. Google became both a blessing and a curse as we dove down one rabbit hole after another, searching for answers. Was it a new medication? Had some strange chemical been introduced to her environment? Was her extreme diet depriving her of some necessary nutrient? Perhaps the years of breathing cat litter had caught up with her? Maybe she had contracted an exotic virus on her last birding expedition? Or was it what the doctors like to term, simply, "cognitive decline"?

She was only seventy-seven.

Years earlier, Mother had written to me, worried about someday being diagnosed with Alzheimer's disease:

> *It may seem silly, but my profile is perfect for it: slightly elevated IQ, no social life at all, no mind exercises like puzzles and such, no physical exercise because of the bad knees, and now back, just what little yard work I can manage but more than anything, solitary confinement, few humans in my life. I find myself groping for verbs I've used all my life—not remembering names is one thing, but ordinary words I've used forever? That scares me. I go back and do actions again because I can't remember doing them or not. I know that some of it is due to stress, trying to cope with everything that's happening, but it is a worry. I can't concentrate when I read. I read sentences over and over. Traffic is becoming scary for me because my mind wanders and I get very tense. I don't know. Maybe I'm just losing the ability to function on anything but a very basic, rote, routine level.*

Mother was an avid reader and, when she wasn't on her knees in the garden or chasing cats around the house, worked her way through piles of magazines and newspapers. More than scanning the headlines, she thoroughly read and processed scads of information. Frequently, she would clip articles, mailing family and friends fun facts and hard truths she deemed noteworthy. It's how her generation communicated about current events. One such piece of mail came to me with a sticky note that read: "I so fear that this is what I have, and I'm scared to death." The article was about Lewy body dementia.

After overhearing yet another scattered conversation one evening, Doug tenderly forced me to face the fact I was trying so hard not to accept: Mother was quickly coming to the place where she would not be able to live in that house alone. Feeling like I had to acknowledge the difficult relationship my mom had with Doug, I said, "I know she hasn't been the warmest person to you or the boys and our family, but I cannot let her die alone." Of course, Doug agreed.

We put pencil to paper and began to do more than imagine what it might look like to move her to the farm.

The Keys

I would like to believe that the embarrassing naked-in-the-driveway scene was a result of some sort of dementia, but that wasn't the case. My mom had several years of independent productivity between that incident and the day I realized she was truly not OK. The day we could no longer chalk up her strange behavior to her eccentric personality. The question now became how to intervene in a way that did not make our already uneasy relationship deteriorate further.

Hesitantly, I began taking steps to intervene in her life, something I had never dared to do before. Most of my efforts backfired, and we now know it was because the disease had progressed further than we could have imagined. On one visit, I took it upon myself to organize her many vitamins and holistic supplements into a pill box. I meticulously moved the capsules from their original bottles into the plastic organizer labeled for not only the day of the week but also the time of day—morning, noon, and evening. Alas, she had become so accustomed to accessing each supplement from its bottle that when

I rearranged them, it challenged her muscle memory to the point of extreme frustration. She could not understand how to get the pills from their new location, so, both of us disheartened to the point of tears, I put them back.

Mother loved music and had quite a record album collection. Songs by Leonard Cohen, Carole King, and Janis Ian had been the soundtrack of her life. Unfortunately, her original turntable had long since ceased to operate. Late that summer, during one of my visits, she glanced wistfully at the albums on the shelf and made an offhand comment, wishing she could listen to them "one last time." Immediately recognizing that fulfilling this desire was something I could do to make her life more pleasant, I began searching for a record player. I found a vintage-style turntable and made a special trip down for her birthday in September to help her set it up. We tried several strategies to teach her how to use it, like tagging in numerical order the components needed to turn it on properly. She never could make it work.

Since her keys appeared to be the flashpoint of so many of her problems, I endeavored to simplify things around the house. The enormous garden and yard were fenced with five locked gates, each with its own key. She would stand at the gate, flipping through the heavy key ring until she lucked upon the right one, and then make her way through to the backyard. It was frustrating for her to experience and even more frustrating to watch. So, on my next visit, I drove to Ace Hardware, purchased new locks, and had them keyed the same. She could exchange the ring of keys with just one that would open everything. I passed the afternoon in the yard, screwdriver in hand, not doubting for a second this would make life easier for Mother. When I finished, we stood in the driveway, and I handed her the single key. "Mom, now you can open all the gates with the same key."

With a furrowed brow and a little panic in her voice, she asked, "Where are my keys?"

"Mom, you don't need the other keys. This one will open all the locks."

More confusion. More panic. My solution had only made things worse. Removing a challenge, no matter how it should have helped, only created distress. She knew where each of her keys went based on its color, shape, and what other key was next to it. When I threw those away, she could not understand how picking up one key would open all the gates. She needed the complex familiar more than the simplified unfamiliar. When she saw my frustration, she began to cry, apologizing for making me mad. Tears gathered in my eyes as well because, at that moment, I realized something very bad was happening to my mother.

The heartbreaking thing? She was lucid enough to know it was too.

Fitting Together Puzzle Pieces

So Mother and I set out in the months following to nail down a diagnosis and, hopefully, a solution. I made the eight-hour drive, time after time, to take her to her family doctor and then to specialists all around the region for lab work, evaluations, and testing. Each visit was fraught with stress as she stewed about what she was going to say and what embarrassing details I might reveal to the doctor. She remained very cognizant, and the part of her that was still there would not allow me to speak for her. Nor did I wish to. During one visit to a psychiatrist who had a dismal bedside manner, Mother called him out for speaking *about* her rather than speaking *to* her. She was still there, able to ask and answer her own questions, and we both let him know it in no uncertain terms. We were not yet ready to swap the parent-child roles that day, but the time to begin that delicate dance would come sooner than we could have guessed.

Owing to the obvious language disorder symptoms she had been experiencing, my mom's initial diagnosis was aphasia. The doctors explained this is a generic term used to define the loss of ability to speak or understand what others are saying. Possible causes include stroke or brain tumor, and we quickly ruled those out. Her normal white blood count also eliminated the possibility of infection being the root of her troubles. An MRI revealed some brain lesions, but nothing was ever said about them contributing to her condition.

One possible diagnosis the doctors floated was early-onset dementia, which sounds like an oxymoron if I've ever heard one.

The search for answers continued.

A turning point arrived during one particularly awful visit for a psychiatric workup in Houston. When the nurse came out to the waiting room and called her name, I looked at Mother, questioning if I should accompany her to the exam room. She shook her head no. That was a mistake. When she eventually exited the room two hours later, she was so frustrated and agitated she was in tears. Turns out a large portion of this testing was word and object recognition and recall, and she had failed miserably. "They just kept asking me the same question over and over again, trying to humiliate me because I didn't understand," she lamented. That was her perception of the previous two hours. Why hadn't I stepped in and asked to observe? I would have recognized her exasperation and pulled her out much earlier. I hated putting her through that and promised she would not face anything like it again. I realized she had lost her ability to advocate for herself and needed to rely on me to be more involved. She was at that torturous point where she knew her thoughts were no longer under her control, yet she remained conscious of them. In hindsight, we know that the disease she was fighting did not take her mind away. Rather, it added hideous images to it, rendering her unable to tell reality from illusion.

What I would learn later was that the "people" she had reported being in the house and outside her window were, in actuality, images in her head. These were not just bad dreams. Her neighbors later told me she had frequently called the police, terrified that someone was trying to break in. She also had visions of my dad, long deceased, sitting at her bedside. Fearing what I might do to intervene, she told me none of this. Yet as the boundary blurred between her lucid thoughts and the horrors that lurked in her subconscious, more of these details came to light. In hindsight, we know these visions were a classic symptom of Lewy body dementia.

Frequently misdiagnosed as Alzheimer's disease or even Parkinson's disease, Lewy body dementia often presents as a combination of cognitive decline, neuromuscular issues, sleep disturbances, and vivid hallucinations. As is true with Parkinson's, all doctors can do is diagnose the disease based on symptoms, observing and narrowing down the scope of possibilities. Definitive diagnosis is only possible during an autopsy. Unlike Parkinson's, the hallucinations begin at the onset of Lewy body dementia rather than presenting at the end stages. According to the Lewy Body Dementia Association, it is the second most common type of dementia. Unfortunately, doctors are only able to diagnose from symptoms patients share, and hallucinations were not something Mother was ready to write down on the intake forms quite yet.

In hindsight, I wish I had given more credence to her stories about the people who visited her at night, making her do unspeakably embarrassing things. She even slept with a stick by the bed as an impotent tool of protection.

The well-meaning doctors always began by explaining that some medications will manifest dementia or Parkinson's symptoms, but Mother would not tolerate wasted time down that path. She never took pills, not even when her doctor advised it. We did learn that a Vitamin B12 deficiency can cause hallucinations. Was that the issue?

Or was it her extreme diet, at that point very low in protein? We were chasing down all kinds of causes in hopes of a cure.

My thoughts drifted to the animal and gardening-related carcinogens she had handled and breathed for her entire life. From the organic fertilizer loaded with bacteria to the chemical additives of her early landscaping days to the copious amounts of kitty litter dust Mother inhaled over the years, it was no wonder her thought processes were being disrupted. I also thought about "those damn petrochemicals" she blamed for all the cancer and strange medical conditions that popped up with increasing frequency along the Texas coast. So the million-dollar questions remained: Were any of these things causing her decline? And if they were, could we figure out how to stop or even reverse it?

As with all types of dementia, early diagnosis and intervention will often slow the loss of independence, with new medications and therapies being introduced regularly. But for someone like Mother, living alone and fiercely independent, the diagnosis came very late. Too late.

Fortunately, in addition to her granting me medical and durable powers of attorney years before, my mom had also recently added me as a signatory on all her accounts. She realized it was a practical thing to do and that, eventually, it would make both of our lives easier. As an only child, it just made sense, but when we went to the bank to complete the paperwork, illogical thoughts of guilt threatened to overtake me. Did these bankers see me as a money-grubbing daughter, not able to wait to get my hands on my mother's estate? Yet by the time we came to this point of desperate exhaustion in pursuit of a diagnosis and treatment, I was so grateful those decisions had been reached, the ink on those documents already dry. Having these legal matters settled made the coming months immeasurably less stressful and painful.

Up to this point, my mom's fierce independence had been the bedrock of our relationship. Now she and I were having worse-case-scenario conversations. The time was obviously coming—soon—when she would require help with daily tasks. We believed we still had some leeway to make and execute a plan. So we talked about the possibility of her moving to the farm with Doug and me or at least relocating closer to us so we could help with her care. "What about my cats?" she asked. Always those damned cats.

Her worst fear was having to enter the nursing home she had watched countless friends and relatives languishing in. She had let me know years before that was not an option she would consider and doubled down on that stance. Mother fretted about her cats, her garden, her house, and how much all this was going to cost, although she had an adequate nest egg that would have covered years of care.

During one particularly raw conversation, both of us in tears, she said, "This is not how it was supposed to be."

"I know, Mom. I know," I replied. "But we don't always get to write the final chapter ourselves."

In true form, my answer was not what she wanted to hear, and in her overwhelmed state, she asked me to leave. I did.

Although Mother was somewhat of a recluse, she was completely committed to taking care of and rehoming cats through the local shelter. Her routine included daily trips to the local facility to drop off kittens, administer medications, clean cages, and answer the phone. This routine would prove to be a lifeline.

Even after her acknowledgment that she was not well, Mother continued to drive. Anyone who has cared for an aging parent knows this is one of the trickiest points you will ever navigate together. When she admitted to me that she sometimes arrived at the shelter but didn't remember driving there, I began to consider how she could continue to live her life without owning a car. Surely, Juaniece could give her a lift each day. I could teach her how to use grocery delivery and ride-sharing apps. (After the key episode, what was I thinking?) There had to be a way to make this work. During one of our phone calls, I began the hard discussion about why she should give up her keys voluntarily. *It couldn't hurt to try*, I reasoned.

"Mother, what if you get lost?" I asked.

"I've been driving these roads my whole life. I'll be fine."

"What if you get hurt?"

"I'll be fine."

"What if you hurt someone else? How could you live with that, Mom?"

Click.

One Friday near the end of October, just two days after she asked me to leave, Mother did not show up as scheduled at the shelter, a move that was very uncharacteristic of her. I'm sure, by this point, her friends were more than aware of her decline, having witnessed the confusion and overall loss of cognitive function on a daily basis. Thankfully, they did not hesitate to jump in their car when she didn't answer the phone. It turns out a norther had blown in, not uncommon on the Texas coast, and temperatures had dropped precipitously overnight. When her friends arrived, it was only fifty degrees in the house. They found her huddled under a pile of blankets, shivering, and completely out of it. She had not been able to remember how to switch the thermostat from air conditioning to heat. My friend Linda, who providentially worked as a home health nurse and routinely checked in on Mother, was called. They decided to bundle Mother up and take her to the ER, and Linda let me know.

Mother would never return home.

CHAPTER 6

The Diagnosis

Even to your old age, I shall be the same, And even to your graying years I shall bear you! I have done it, and I shall carry you; And I shall bear you, and I shall deliver you.

—Isaiah 46:4, NASB

IT WOULD GIVE me great pride and pleasure to report that my thoughts were focused on Mother after that jarring phone call from Linda. I started out with some positivity: *Thank you, Lord, for prompting someone to go check on Mother when she didn't show up for work. Praise you for providing me with reliable transportation, a supportive husband, and a flexible job. Thank you for being here with me.* But eventually, a mighty intense pity party broke out in my head that afternoon. Could you blame me? I had just left Port Lavaca a couple days before, clearly expressing my belief that Mother should not be living alone—butting heads on that and so many other issues. Of course, I felt the weight of expectation, mostly self-inflicted, that I would jump in the car and head immediately the eight hours back to her house, but I resisted.

Linda, who had witnessed countless rocky moments between Mother and me, served not only as my eyes and ears at the hospital but also as a gauge for my heart, assuring me it was OK to take care of myself first, just like the flight attendants tell us to do. Linda became my medical sanity check, a golden link to the inner workings of the Port Lavaca health care system. She was, and is, a priceless treasure. After talking to the doctors, Linda was convinced Mother would be discharged in a day or two. So I waited until Sunday to drive down, arriving late, and after checking on those damn cats, fled to the shelter of Linda's house.

We too often confuse acquaintances with friends, but they are altogether different categories. Unless you have that once-in-a-lifetime true friend, I don't think you understand the difference, but Linda was, and is, that friend to me. In school, we walked parallel paths. She was in choir, and I was in band. She was on the dance team, and I most certainly was not. She went to nursing school at the University of Texas, and I went to engineering college at Texas A&M University. We saw each other occasionally but not frequently because we both got busy raising our families. Yet Linda was the friend who, when I was in need, opened her home to me. On those evenings when I would come back from taking care of Mother, we would curl up on her couch, wine in hand, talking about anything and everything. It was like we never lost a moment in time.

I Cannot Live Like This

Monday morning came too soon, and I found myself, once again, in the Memorial Medical Center parking lot. Memories of Daddy and even Paw-Paw in this place flooded my mind; sadness and death permeated those halls. Would more grief be born here before long? I pushed those thoughts aside, took a deep breath, and pushed on. When I entered Mother's room, she seemed relieved to see me, compounding the guilt I felt for taking two days to arrive. I sat by her side on the bed where she was propped up, looking like someone ready to go home. I put my hand in hers, and the next moment seemed surreal, even in our weird little world.

Mother looked me in the eye, brow furrowed, intent on getting every word just right, and said, "I cannot live like this. I want you to help me kill myself."

What? I thought. *Surely, I hadn't heard that right.* But I had. It simultaneously took my breath away and broke my heart.

"Oh, Mom, you know I can't do that."

Deflated, she laid back on the pillow and said, "I knew you'd say that."

Then I made my first promise: "Mom, I can't help you end your life, but I can do this: I know the things you absolutely do not want done to you, and I promise not to let anyone do those things." She knew I was referring to her wish not to have her life prolonged by artificial means. We had discussed those things over the years, and her desires were clear.

That bit of emotional housekeeping aside, we set out to navigate the circus known as the American health-care system.

The Lists

I must stop here and say how overwhelmingly grateful I am for those who devote their careers and lives to caring for others with medical issues. The doctors—no matter how frustrating some of them can be—who answer the phone in the middle of the night and show up no matter what is going on in their own families. The nurses who miss holidays and their kids' special events to administer solutions to the sick and injured. The aides, especially those in memory care and hospice roles, who croon comforting words and clean up messes. The world is a better place because they are in it.

Like Maw-Maw, my mom was a list-maker. True to form, she then pulled out scraps of paper, in her now very illegible handwriting, with details about everything I needed to know if she were to become completely unable to communicate—or worse. Thankfully, she was cognizant enough to realize those important facts could slip through her fingers at any moment. She struggled mightily to explain "things." Where were her insurance files? What Medicare supplements did she have? Where was the key to her safe deposit box? We didn't broach the subject of her house, both assuming she would be returning there in a matter of hours or at least days.

The hospital social worker was another true godsend. She sat patiently with me during countless meetings, my introduction to the complex world of Medicare, explaining terminology and exploring options. Skilled nursing services, coverage restrictions, managed care, donut holes—the learning curve was steep, but I had no choice. As my mind whirled, making decisions while totally trusting the hospital staff to give sound advice, I felt woefully inept and ill-informed. What I chose from this medical smorgasbord was going to profoundly impact my mother, her recovery, and her quality of life. How could I be sure these decisions made would be in her best interest? I couldn't. But I could rely on God to give me wisdom. He had never failed me yet.

One plan we discussed was for her to return home and either continue to live alone with regular home health intervention or hire someone trustworthy to stay with her full-time, which is easier said than done, especially with the tiny labor pool available in a small town like Port Lavaca. My job was to figure out how to make one of those options happen without draining her bank account. Medicare, unfortunately, does not pay for full-time in-home care or long-term nursing home care, so that looming cost would have to be covered from her savings. Aside from the questionable expense of housing dozens of cats, my mom was a savvy spender and intentional saver, living solely on her social security benefits even though she had an adequate amount of money in the bank. She wasn't rich by any means, but I hate to think of how her options would have been limited if she had no cushion.

At that time, Doug and I still believed the best solution was for her to move to the farm, perhaps living in a tiny house to maintain her independence. We were just taking that one step at a time and hadn't really begun to figure out the logistics of not only the move but also covering her daily care while we both continued working full-time, traveling often.

So Monday passed, and then Tuesday, wall-to-wall with meetings and appointments, but Mother was still not stable enough to return home. I kissed her goodbye that night, whispering hope that she might be discharged in the morning.

Then morning came.

And the whole world changed.

That Horrible Wednesday

As I walked past the nurses' station that Wednesday, bright and early in hopes of being there when the doctor made his rounds, one of the nurses stopped me with a word of warning. They had experienced a long night of Mother being combative and generally uncooperative, and things were deteriorating quickly. I rushed into the room and skidded to a stop at the sight. The woman in the bed was not the same one I had kissed the night before. With two or three nurses trying to restrain her, my mom was fighting a very real battle with the horrific images her mind was conjuring. Thrashing as she threw punches to stop rats and headless people from clawing her eyes out, kicking and ducking to escape monsters threatening from every corner of the room, completely out of control and in a state of abject terror. What she was describing was like a scene from *The Walking Dead*. There are no words to adequately portray the pathetic state she was in. The nurses were doing their best, but it seemed that even the standard sedatives they had administered seemed to actually increase her agitation.

The doctor had been summoned, but those who have experienced a true medical emergency can testify that time stands still as you wait for the person who might be able to alter the mad circumstances in which you found yourself. As Mother's flailing was not abating, I called Linda. "Something horrible is happening to Mother. Can you come?" Thankfully, within minutes, she arrived, filling the void until the doctor could get there. Finally, he arrived.

After examining Mother and administering some antipsychotic drugs, which at length calmed her down, the doctor, nurses, Linda, and I all took a breath. As we stood at the nurses' station, the doctor made the definitive diagnosis of Lewy body dementia. He told us it was a textbook case of the disease, confirmed by the precipitous change in behavior. This was not a gradual decline, he warned, like something you'd expect with normal dementia or Parkinsons. It was not something that would get better. She had fallen off a cliff.

"Lewy body dementia is the dementia from hell," he pronounced. Truer words were never spoken.

He offered to do more testing. I declined. Mother had diagnosed herself correctly years before.

During this day, this horrible Wednesday, I remember walking the halls of the hospital, crying uncontrollably. What had just the day before seemed like a situation I could manage, plans in hand, had spun out of control with a stunning finality. One of those wise, experienced caregivers suggested Mother might be comforted by holding something familiar. Perhaps a stuffed cat. Desperately needing something to do, a concrete contribution I could make, I headed to the hospital gift shop in search of the perfect kitty. As I scanned the shelves, my head began to spin, my eyes losing focus. Falling to my knees in despair, I wailed: "I cannot believe I'm here looking for a damned stuffed animal for my mother!"

Port Lavaca is a small community, so I assume the poor auxiliary ladies, older volunteers, knew my mother. Like the other dedicated caregivers in that building, I'm sure they had seen it all—the profound joy of the new daddy choosing flowers for his wife who had just given birth to their dream and the raw agony of those who had lost or were about to lose a precious loved one. Those tender-hearted women attempted to provide comfort, but I was inconsolable. Throughout the coming months, even during the last days of Mother's life on earth, nothing compared to the grief that consumed me that day. The gravity of the situation finally pressed so hard it was not to be ignored any longer. Everything had changed. I would not be bringing Mother home; in fact, she would never go home again.

So we shifted to Plan B. And by the end of the process, we had considered and discarded so many plans that I'm not sure where we landed in the alphabet. During those days, the stress and fatigue created more than one instance where I doubted even my own cognitive abilities would ever be the same. The doctor and social worker were insistent that Mother not return home alone, and there was no argument from her or me about that call. It would only be a matter of days before some horrific vision twisted her mind enough to burn the house down or wander off down the beach (naked, of course). Since we hadn't had time to prepare a place for her at our farm, the only option, a temporary one in my mind, was to move Mother to a nursing home.

The one place she told me she never wanted to be.

We had no other choice.

This is where I learned that you can't expect to have exactly what you need available when and where you need it, even in this great country of ours. Even if you have money. The tradeoff with a small, supportive community like Port Lavaca is there are not many options for skilled nursing care. When the day came that Mother was required to be discharged from the hospital—*thank you, Medicare*—there were no rooms available in the memory care unit of the only long-term care facility in town. There was a bed on the standard, nonsecure floor, and that was the choice we had.

"Who will stay with her?" I asked. She was in no shape to be left alone. They told me kindly that I could sit at her bedside or hire someone else to. I don't remember how long she had to wait for a spot in memory care, but it was too long.

The goal was to move her into the local nursing home while I searched for a facility closer to my house. I had nightmares about how we would transport her that four hundred miles down the highway. What if she started to hallucinate during the drive and tried to jump from the car or grab the steering wheel? How would I manage pit stops? And what if, heaven forbid, we had car trouble? Those dusty Texas roads were no place for a dementia-riddled old lady and her overwhelmed daughter.

Turns out, all those worries were wasted energy, as I soon learned that special licensing was required for nursing homes to dispense the heavy antipsychotic drugs Mother needed. The closest facility that ticked all the boxes was more than an hour from our home, not exactly a place I could run over to every day to monitor how she was doing.

In the end, Doug and I decided it would be best for her to stay in Port Lavaca, where she could at least benefit from her friends' visits. And with Linda's unofficial oversight of the situation, it was a comfort to know she was there. Mother's friend Juaniece visited every single day. She not only ensured Mom was receiving good care but also delivered snacks and toiletries and, most importantly, lifted her spirits.

This gut-wrenching turn of events put me in the weird space where many children of aging parents find themselves. How do I let my mother's friends and our extended family know what has taken place? Or, even more precisely, do I tell them at all? Would Mother want everyone to hear about her inability to turn on the furnace—her struggle to maintain a simple string of thoughts? Or would she rather slip into obscurity with the community of Port Lavaca wondering what had happened to her? After reading some of the things she left behind, as heartbreaking as it is to consider, I don't think she believed anyone but the cats would miss her when she was gone.

So, as much as needing a way to chronicle and process the previous unthinkable few months as anything, I wrote and mailed Mother's annual Christmas letter.

> *To say that things have changed dramatically for Mother in a bad way is an understatement. As I write this, please understand that she has become the person and finds herself in the place that she never wanted to be. We don't always get to write the final chapter with the ending we want. I never imagined drafting a letter like this at this early stage of her life.*
>
> *Mother still knows her friends. I was there this last weekend, and she knew me but didn't believe it was me—thought "they" were trying to trick her. Her world is a mixture of lucidity and hallucinations. She still wants to control the things around her, and that is much of what torments her. I wish there was something happy or positive that I could share, but there just isn't.*

> *I thank you for the friendship you have shown Mother over the years. Only you and her know the true depth and value of that. Now, I simply ask that you pray for her.*

I know now, with all of my heart, people were praying. And God was listening, prepared to grant us a yes regarding our petitions for Mother's soul.

CHAPTER 7

Too Soon

*I have seen everything that is done under the sun;
and behold, all is vanity and a striving after wind.*

—*Ecclesiastes 1:14*

O N THE EVE of her sixty-ninth birthday, Mother had sent me what I would term a warning. A poignant list of advice about how I someday would be slammed with the reality of aging as she had been. She included a newspaper clipping containing some nuggets of wisdom I cannot recall. Then, couched in simple terms, she described an epiphany she had experienced about how things were bound to be markedly different by the end of her next ten years, or her "last chance decade." Of course, she believed I would be unable to relate, and she was correct, but it was imperative for her to illustrate her vision for what we both assumed would be her final productive years. Mother laid out the "distinctive decade" this way:

> *A decade of getting ready, tying up loose ends if possible, seeing far too many of one's own age in the obits each day, a true feeling of living on borrowed time that has not existed before, as we have always lived for 'when' and 'then,' and constantly moving forward to goals. Now the goals are so very different; quite a feeling, dear heart.*

She went on to inventory her many regrets: failing to grasp how her mother's end-of-life fears were not simply "needless worrying"; being unable to travel because of her overwhelming pet responsibilities; becoming so worn out that she no longer cared about the yard ("a shattering thing"); and, of course, her failure as a grandmother.

But the words that were burned in my brain were about her own end-of-life care. She was fused to that house after sixty years, and the thought of giving up the peace that came with controlling her environment was more than she could bear. Some people have conversations or unspoken understandings that they don't want to end up in a nursing home, but Mother spelled it out, using Maw-Maw's long-term care placement as a vivid example:

> *I would ask that you not place me in a nursing home unless my mind is gone, for then what happens to the body is irrelevant. The world is hurtling at warp speed toward its destruction because of greed and excess, and my one small plot of refuge is but a tiny speck in the scheme of things. I want to stay here, in this place, for as long as I can manage, even if that means crawling around on my hands and knees to get things done. I can't imagine anyone taking care of me, all the indignities that a helpless body makes possible.*

> *Despite all the good aspects that I felt I was seeing (in the nursing home), things being done for Mother, staff who truly cared about her, it was the cruelest thing I ever did to her, ugly beyond belief.*

Ugly beyond belief. Yet here we were, the one place she never wanted to be.

A New Normal

Once we determined that moving Mother north to our area would not be in her best interest, I set up a loose two-week visiting schedule. Those hours on the road, as much as I dreaded being away from home, turned out to be good therapy. Providing a haven to decompress from work, catch up with the kids over the phone, and fill my spiritual well through prayer time and sing-a-longs, those drives turned out to be fruitful. Linda continued to shower me with her gift of hospitality, and it was always so helpful to talk through things with someone who knew the system and understood the intricacies of the singular relationship between my mother and me.

I selected a few things from Mother's home in the hope that they would make her feel more comfortable and grounded to reality in the new environment: a portable CD player, which she was never able to operate; her laptop to watch her favorite shows, which she never used. I even grabbed a beautiful little tan-and-brown handwoven basket she had brought home from one of her South American birding trips and put it on her bedside table to hold her Chapstick. It disappeared the first night. Later, one of her handmade afghans suffered a similar fate.

Most of my visits were short, as I quickly discovered the staggering emotional toll of seeing what this disease had reduced my mom to.

Watching other patients in the common area of the memory care unit muttering or yelling just made me sad.

In addition to the ongoing mental decline, my mom's small frame reacted with extreme lethargy to the antipsychotic drugs. One day, I took a photo of her looking bedraggled and forlorn while sitting at a table in the dining room. She never liked having her picture taken, and I felt a little guilty about it, knowing she would have hated it. But I knew someday I would need to better process this pain, to have a bare-faced reminder of what things had really been like, so I tucked it away.

Even with the antipsychotics, my mom's delusions did not abate. On more than one occasion, she mentioned "the rats." At mealtime, she would take a bite, then cover her plate with a napkin "so that rat won't get the food and run away with it." During one visit, I picked up a sock that had been kicked under a dresser. She told me the rats had put it there.

At this point in the disease progression, paranoia had been woven tightly throughout her mind. To her, the threat from people in the hall and outside the window was very real. From time to time, we would be having what I assumed was a normal conversation, and she would shush me, warning that "they" would hear. She feared "they" would kidnap her, make her stand on a stage, and take her clothes off before they cut her. I once tried to reassure her there was no one in the hall who intended to harm her. She refused my comfort, shouting, "I know you are telling me they are not there, but *I cannot differentiate what is real from what is not real!*"

This was not the language of a crazy woman whose mind was gone, but rather the pathetic confession of someone still rational enough to realize her thoughts had been invaded by unreal images and horrors. I think that is what the doctor meant when he called Lewy body dementia "the dementia from hell."

Between visits, I would call to talk to the nurses about how Mother was doing. We discussed doing a FaceTime call, which was a nice suggestion but not something my mom and I had ever done before. In her confused state, I was afraid things would not go well. The nurses were endlessly patient and kind, telling me if it was a good or bad day and describing what she was up to. One day, they reported she was crawling down the hallway, and that wretched scene threatened to destroy me. Linda suggested perhaps this was a result of Mother's muscle memory comforting her, a reminder of countless hours on her hands and knees in the garden and caring for the cats. I wanted to believe it was a therapeutic exercise allowing her to return to happier days, but, realistically, it was most likely another manifestation of those horrible hallucinations that plagued her relentlessly.

As is common with Lewy body dementia, Mother began to frequently fall out of bed while thrashing around in battles with the invisible images she fought against while trying to sleep. Eventually, they placed her mattress on the floor. I hope that provided a smidgen of familiarity. A glimpse of how things were at home. But it was hard to watch.

In order to meet all the requirements of Medicare, I was required to participate in periodic meetings with staff to discuss Mother's progress and care plan. One meeting that stood out was with the physical therapist bemoaning the fact he was not able to convince Mother to participate in an activity where they all sat in a circle and threw a beach ball to each other. I did my best to explain that her belligerence was no surprise. She would not have agreed to such a childish game on her best days, so we couldn't expect her to do it now. Please don't ask her to.

The Storage Container

Adult children of aging parents understand that, once Mother entered the nursing home, we were stopped at yet another crossroads. It was time to face the truth that she was not going to get better. She would die either in a bed in the nursing home or one at the hospital, not on a pallet in her beloved house surrounded by kitties, not on a mountain, chasing an elusive bird through the rainforest. Mother had given up hope of ever traveling again, but she continued to cling, understandably, to the belief she would return home someday. Her doctors and my common sense said otherwise. There was nothing I could do about her thoughts, but I could control how things were handled regarding her stuff. It was time to get to work.

Every day, I thanked God that my mom had already given me official permission to make medical and financial decisions. Having to go through another suffocating pile of paperwork while dealing with her continuing struggles would have been too much.

In a small town, word gets out quickly when a house is sitting empty, tempting vandals and vagrants alike. It was time to deal with the physical aftermath of sixty years of life. Somehow, we had to get her things securely stored. We considered using a local storage unit, but the gulf coast humidity would have made a mess of that in short order. With the approval of our accountant, Doug and I came up with a plan to purchase a forty-foot container van and park it on our property. Then, after packing up the house and paying movers to get it to us, we planned to shove everything in there and take a breath before deciding what to do with it all. And I could tell Mother, truthfully, that her things were all intact and being well cared for. This I would do after the fact, praying I could present it as a *fait accompli*, laying out the logic that it was the best thing to do. Thankfully, that strategy worked.

My sister-in-law, Jeanne, an absolute angel on earth, offered to help. Facing her own stressors and the regular grind of life, she didn't think twice about driving to Port Lavaca with me and packing boxes. I could not have done it without her.

Jeanne and I established a few rules, including a prohibition on looking through anything. No opening photo albums or files, no questioning whether something should be tossed out or given away. Just fill the boxes. At one point, when I was running one of a dozen essential errands on Mother's behalf, Jeanne called to say she had just opened a kitchen cupboard overflowing with old plastic containers. We agreed that some things really did deserve a spot in the landfill. Even though nothing would have brought me more joy than Mother being lucid enough to ask where her margarine containers had gone, that scenario was clearly beyond the realm of possibility. She was not coming home.

Proof of my mom's sentimentality remained: Handmade cards I had given her when I was little, mementos of her own childhood, and literally hundreds of gorgeous books on birding and gardening gathered dust on shelves and in drawers. Later, I found treasure troves of family history, including my dad's Purple Heart, and definitive proof we were descended from American patriots. Jeanne and I wrapped dozens of framed photos from Mother's travels. We threw files in specially marked boxes to be sorted through with top priority when the time came. That elusive day in the future when I could not only carve the hours from my schedule but also summon the emotional energy to look back.

One of the biggest surprises came as Jeanne was emptying a junk drawer in Mother's buffet. Among the odds and ends, such as screws, batteries, and picture hangers, was a pill bottle labeled "Lyman's Ashes." Apparently, she had saved a little souvenir from her trip to Banff with Daddy's friends to scatter his ashes. Jeanne and I got quite a kick out of that, wondering what in the world she had been thinking and what in the world we were supposed to do with them. So, after sharing a stress-relieving belly laugh, following our own self-imposed rule, into a box they went.

Proof of my mom's over-the-top frugality also remained. In addition to never throwing away a plastic tub, it looked like she hadn't bought new underwear in years. When I opened that drawer of threadbare underthings, the sight immediately took me back to the aunties, who had a different set of panties for home and for "going to town" because you never knew if you were going to get in a car accident and have your clothes cut off by the paramedics. Old clothes that I would have just thrown away, Mother cut up for cleaning rags. Hundreds of plastic grocery store bags spilled from one cupboard. Clothes flapped on the line in the backyard because she had long ago quit using her dryer, saving both money and Mother Earth.

Once the house was cleaned out, there was still the yard to contend with. As I stepped out the back door on our final day of packing, a cold mist greeted me—as if the garden itself was grieving the loss of its caretaker. Mother loved her outdoor spaces and their contents as much as anything inside, and I knew she would hold me accountable for each special rock and birdhouse. So I found the wheelbarrow and got to work. I hadn't intended on employing the "pack-everything" mentality in the yard. However, after a few hours of culling, the driveway was filled with one-of-a-kind stones, yard ornaments, antique wrought-iron gates, and wayside benches, each carrying my mother's spirit with them somehow. I could not leave them behind.

Most of the outdoor décor fit in the moving van, but a couple weeks later, I rented a Dodge three-quarter-ton pickup, drove it to Port Lavaca, and began filling it—really filling it— with the remaining rocks and stones. *Just one more*, I would think. *Oh, I have to take this cool one.* It's a wonder I didn't have a blowout driving home.

Since then I've managed to construct a little stone patio at my house with Mother's collection. Once when we were sitting outside, Doug commented that he saw what I had done. When I questioned what that meant, he replied that I had made a memorial garden for my mom. I suppose I had. This year, I plan to use her wrought-iron gates to delineate a little pet cemetery. She would have loved it. I know I do.

The next problem to be tackled was her cats. At that point, she had eight or ten cats living inside the house and about the same number outside. Juaniece and Mother's other friends at the shelter got busy thoughtfully rehoming those fur babies to new owners best suited for each one. Knowing the idiosyncrasies and needs of each cat were being carefully considered brought Mother a measure of comfort. Eventually, a pair of siblings, brother and sister, remained. They were living outside, so I decided to adopt them myself, hoping they would enjoy joining our menagerie at the farm.

Mother had very firm notions about the type of person she wanted me to sell her house to when the time came. A couple that lived behind her was of like mind with Mother in using their yard as a wildlife habitat, and she asked they have first right of refusal on one of the lots. Her great fear was that the sale of her property would result in a trailer park going in next to them, destroying all the beauty they were creating. She advised me against selling to the first person one of those "horrible, greedy, heartless realtors" showed the house to.

In stark contrast to Mother's view of greedy realtors, her former employer offered to list the house, waiving his commission. He recommended we get a "little landscaping" done, just trim some things up so someone could pull into the driveway and see the front door or make it up the sidewalk without tripping. I agreed. Mother's natural habitat had gotten out of hand. So he hired a crew and the work was done. The next week, when I drove around the corner and looked up, I couldn't believe my eyes. They had chain sawed everything. It looked like someone had bombed it with Agent Orange. Nothing was left.

I wept.

The realtor assured me that it had not been his intention to destroy the yard, but what could we do? My only consolation was that Mother never had to see it. She would have died a thousand deaths knowing the results of her decades of tender loving care and master gardening—homes and sustenance for birds, bugs, and butterflies—had been obliterated in an afternoon.

Mother grew more and more frail at each visit but was still very able to communicate. When I would walk in the door, she had a list in hand detailing all the things she wanted to tell me. During one visit, she asked if I would take her, just one more time, to walk through her house. "I promise to be good," she pleaded. She desperately needed to see and touch some of her favorite things, to say goodbye to those keepsakes and the memories they represented.

By this time, her house had long been emptied out. I could have hedged, putting the discussion off for another visit or telling her we would go over later, but I decided to be straight with her. Deftly walking the tightrope of explaining that things would not be how she remembered them because I had moved them to take care of them for her. She didn't argue or cry. After considering my explanation, she took on a look of resolute acceptance. *It is what it is*, I could hear her thinking.

During that visit, as she struggled to make her way through the list, Mother broached the subject of how to let her friends know what was happening to her. That's when I told her about the Christmas letter I had sent. I held my breath as she processed the news, but she simply smiled peacefully and said, "I knew you'd take care of it." In tears, I read her the letter and some of the replies she had received.

Another thing on her list that day was money. She was worried about the mounting cost of her care, fearing it would take everything she had saved, not leaving anything for me and my boys. I assured I had done the math, and she had plenty to live on, and she didn't owe us any money.

That visit was one of the longest we had, and as I would share with Doug while driving home, it felt like God had blessed me with what might become my last best couple hours with her. It was February of 2020, and life as we knew it was about to change for us all.

CHAPTER 8

The Final Days

Behold, now is the acceptable time; behold, now is the day of salvation.

—*2 Corinthians 6:2b*

THE NEXT FEW months of COVID lockdown were hard. Although some families opted for FaceTime or visiting through a window, in Mother's state of mind, that would have been horribly confusing. My only option was to call the nurses often to check in. Even Juaniece and Linda were unable to visit her. Every day, I wondered what was going through my mom's mind. Did she realize it had been weeks, then months, since she'd had a visitor? Was she lonely? Or did one day just run into the next? I also struggled with guilt when I realized it was actually a relief not to have to make that long drive and face the ugliness of her disease.

At the end of April, I got the call that Mother had been admitted to the hospital due to mild pneumonia and a blood infection. Hospital visitors remained forbidden, so I stayed connected through daily phone calls with the nurses, whose responsibilities had expanded from health care to include remote communications management. They truly were my heroes.

After months of lockdown, Doug and I were desperately missing our boys, daughters-in-law, and our sweet baby granddaughters, so the weekend before Mother's Day, we gathered for an early celebration, masks in hand, at our son Paul's house in East Texas. My heart stopped when my phone began to chime—it always did at this point in Mother's journey—and I had to sit down when I saw the hospital number on my screen. Part of me wished I could instruct those medical callers to lead with, "She's not dead," before they said anything else. Once I determined Mother was indeed still alive, the news was as dire as could be. The doctor reported that although Mother was responding to the antibiotics prescribed for the pneumonia, she had reached the end stages of Lewy body dementia. He compassionately recommended beginning palliative care through hospice, and he let me know she would likely not be going back to the nursing home. Isn't it strange how the best news I could have had at this point was her return to the place we both had dreaded for so long?

It took about a week to work through the approval process that allowed me to visit her in the hospital. Lockdown protocols at that point were both rigid and fluid, if that makes any sense. No one had a solid frame of reference for decision-making, and recommendations changed on what seemed like a daily if not hourly basis. Thankfully, it was determined Mother would not have to die alone.

The Long Drive

By this point, Doug was dealing with some serious health issues of his own. Coupling that with the ongoing farm responsibilities, we decided it was best I make that final trip to Port Lavaca without him. Our children were busy starting their own families and working new jobs, so I told them not to come. I felt this was mine to do. I told Doug I didn't know how long I'd be gone, but I planned to stay until the end.

Friday afternoon, I arrived at the hospital. An empty grocery store bag blew across the deserted visitor parking lot. The gift shop where I had my breakdown just a few short months before was dark, the door locked tight, trinkets and stuffed animals gathering dust. The hallways were eerily quiet as I made my way to Mother's door. She was in bed, the curtains drawn, and I walked over to give her a kiss. She looked up and smiled with recognition. "Your hair looks pretty," she said. *This really is* The Twilight Zone, I thought. Mother would normally comment on my hair, but not by giving positive feedback.

She was well past writing lists of things to discuss with me, but our stilted conversation kept circling back to "the book." It was at the forefront of her thoughts and obviously a very important message she wanted to get across to me.

"Finish the book. Get it published," she repeated.

I had no idea what she meant, but after a long volley on this topic, I acquiesced. "OK, Mom, I will."

The first thing I learned from the nurse was that Mother got extremely agitated when they came to transport her for any procedures. I remember looking around the room at the staff, covered from head to foot in protective garb, double-masked, and wearing respirators that rendered them barely recognizable as human. "No wonder," I told them. "You all look like the monsters she has been hallucinating about."

The second thing I learned that day is that end-of-life wishes, no matter how clearly they are expressed before the fact, are a sticky wicket. Mother had told me she did not want life-saving measures to be taken if she were ever in the position we found ourselves at that moment. The doctor explained that the antibiotics being used to treat the pneumonia and blood infection were indeed keeping her alive. Is that what I wanted? Once again, I could not see the path ahead, and someone was asking me to take a step from which there would be no return. No take-backs.

The decision became easier when he explained that allowing the infection to run rampant would cause her to die in extreme pain. That was not what she would have wanted. The treatment continued.

Day Two

What followed was the day of reckoning for Mother that I described in the introduction of this book. Although by the end we experienced a little relief, the anxiety preceding her surrender to Christ was practically unbearable. Mother had experienced a sleepless night, babbling about people hurting her. The torturous thing is that when she wasn't reacting to invisible threats, she was very much with it. I would ask her to try to close her eyes and rest. She would affirm her intention of doing so and then fail to. When I repeated myself, she said, "I heard you the first time. You don't need to keep repeating yourself."

By midafternoon, things had not improved. I texted Doug:

> *This is such a living hell for her. She has been almost twenty-four hours with no sleep. Not even after the morphine. They just gave her another dose. She just stares at things and talks nonstop—everything from trees to money to shoes to*

people I don't know. Constantly trying to finish something and very upset because she cannot.

She called out to dead family members as the desperation ratcheted up higher than I had ever seen it. That was when the counting started. Her reprimand that my Jesus was not present and my insistence he was. The spiritual warfare taking place in that room was enough to convince the most belligerent atheist they require the advocacy and protection of a savior. Evil was looming. But God was bigger.

I often chuckle, wondering what the hospital staff would have thought if someone had walked in on Mother's spiritual standoff with me blubbering over her. Thankfully, they gave us privacy.

After Mother's declaration for Christ, there was no whoosh of wind being sucked from the room, no harp music that we could hear—although the Bible tells us in Luke 15:10 the angels were rejoicing. But from that moment on, there was peace, her anxiety greatly reduced and demeanor increasingly relaxed. In the days to come my mom would talk to people I knew were waiting to greet her in heaven. Her mother, who was a strong and faithful woman, her grandmother, her brother. She called out the names of Aunt Alma and Uncle Louis and others in my grandmother's generation. It was as if God was saying, "Here's what's in front of you, Gloria, my precious daughter. This is your future."

Mother's transition in those moments was stark, shifting suddenly from anxiety, senseless hallucinations, spastic movements, and trying to get things done to a peacefulness and assurance of a future in paradise.

This is what carried me through the next eight days as she moved closer and closer to eternity. As I reflected on the journey, realizing all that needed to be done had been done. Nothing more needed to happen. The disease still had her in its grip, and hard days were to follow, but now she was assured of a final destination where a host of other saints awaited her admittance.

Day Three

In the midst of all the heavy emotions surrounding the deathbed of a loved one, life goes on. It's those moments of humor that help keep you grounded, a reminder there are people who love and need you. Before sunrise that third day, Doug texted, asking how to operate the coffee maker. Then, later, a request for instructions on operating the dishwasher. *How do I make fried rice? How long should I cook these frozen sausages?* Each question was punctuated with encouraging blessings like *I love you. You are a precious mother, daughter, and wife*!

Life goes on.

I had forgotten it was Mother's Day, but Doug encouraged me to take myself out for a nice meal. *Thanks! I had McDonald's for lunch—does that count*? I replied. I really was fine. Just so relieved that Mother was resting peacefully. I suppose that's what ridding oneself of demons and welcoming the Holy Spirit will do for you. When she did wake up that afternoon, she began calling out to Jesus.

Jesus!

What joy filled my soul.

Another stark difference about lockdown protocols in the hospital was a lack of clergy. When I mentioned this to Linda, she asked if I would like her Catholic priest to come pray with us. I said, "Absolutely, I need all the prayers I can get. This is hard." Turns out, this young man actually knew Mother, and we joked about the joys of small-town living. I shared with him what had happened to Mother and her new hope of heaven, even though I acknowledged it didn't align with his faith. But he was very comforting, agreeing that it was not a time to get caught up in the details but rather to rejoice in the fact she had embraced forgiveness in Christ. To be thankful that we can know we will be reunited with our loved ones someday. Then he prayed a beautiful prayer. I told him it would have made any Baptist preacher proud, and we laughed together. He left me with a small crucifix, which I tucked away to be buried with Mother's ashes.

Day Four

At this point, I was beginning to think perhaps I do too much for my husband. The texts continued, each one bringing a smile to my face:
Are we out of soy?
Where is my scarf?
Do you have the body shop guy's name and number?
Life goes on. It's good to smile, to be needed.

And that day, I needed all the smiles I could get. Late afternoon, the doctor announced they would be moving Mother back to the nursing home—*thanks again, Medicare*. That news was startling enough, but then we discovered her room in the memory care unit was no longer available. She was transported, once again, onto the regular floor, where the staff was unable to administer the antipsychotic drugs Mother so desperately needed. On top of that, hospice did not provide twenty-four-hour care. So the nurse told me I could stay with Mother in her room. What? Was she kidding? I panicked.

Once again, God sent an angel on earth to my rescue. When the hospice nurse arrived, she saw the panic on my face and, after checking things out, realized the accommodations would not work well in Mother's case, not because the staff was unsympathetic but because of narcotics regulations. She gave me the option to move Mother to a hospice facility in Victoria, a town about thirty miles up the road, where they could better manage her physical discomfort and anxiety. Her blood infection persisted, and the nurse reiterated the doctor's previous message that it would be a painful way to die without the right interventions. I looked at my mom, so frail and helpless, wondering what to do. What was this hospice facility like? Would she even survive the trip? I had been thrown onto this path in a world I didn't know, taking one step at a time and hoping not to make the wrong choice. *Lord, help me*, I prayed in desperation. Finally, after discussing things with Doug and Linda, I decided to move her to Victoria. While the nurse made the arrangements for her transportation, I went back in to sit with Mother.

For reasons I cannot explain, my mom held very liberal views on things. Perhaps that is one reason she struggled with the Bible. We simply agreed to disagree on politics, but that night, I was the one with the remote. I had *The Sean Hannity Show* on Fox News, volume down, and I didn't even think she was awake enough to realize what was going on when I heard, "Blabber, blabber, blabber." I burst out laughing, relieving a sliver of the day's stress.

It was nearing midnight when we had the most precious conversation. Struggling to get the words from her brain to her tongue, she said, "Your family—all good—so sorry," acknowledging what she had missed out on, what could have been such a special part of her life. Perhaps my boys, now men, who never understood why she wasn't the grandmother we thought she should be, can find solace in that confession.

Day Five

Juaniece had beat me up to Mother's room at Hospice of South Texas the next day. Unable to visit since lockdown began, she realized the hospice lockdown rules were a bit more relaxed than other health-care facilities, and she took full advantage of it. By the end of the day, two more of Mother's friends from the shelter had stopped by. They told me that, on more than one occasion, Mother had shown them pictures of our granddaughters. She had talked about our daughter-in-law being pregnant and lamented she would never meet any of the babies. Mother had never told me those things, so it was nice to hear that, in her own way, family did matter.

My worries about the quality of care in Victoria were more than unfounded. This five-star facility provided comfort and compassion beyond my wildest expectations. I did, however, have to learn a new set of rules for that setting. One of the great things was that Medicare would pick up one hundred percent of hospice care costs.

From the beautiful room and picture window overlooking a manicured lawn that led to a little creek to the comfortable furnishings that were nicer than anything Mother had ever owned, it was just perfect. The first nurse to see her began implementing an entire regimen of personal care, stating she was going to bathe Mother, wash her hair, and cut her nails. When I said I didn't think her nails were too bad, the woman tsk-tsked and said, "No one under my care is going to heaven with nails like that." Finally, I could relax, knowing these important things were being taken care of.

My introduction to the process of letting my mother die soon came. They brought one meal, and I tried over the course of a whole shift to get her to swallow something. When the night nurse came on, I asked how hard I should try to get her to eat. With great compassion, she looked at me, picked up the tray, and said, "She won't eat again."

The patient advocate asked how I felt about Mother being heavily sedated. She explained that was the only way she could be completely comfortable, but often, families do not want that level of sedation because there are final conversations that still need to happen. I told her my mom and I had already had the last, best, and most meaningful conversation we needed. There was nothing else left to be said.

My only panic at that outstanding facility occurred when the social worker casually tossed out the phrase "when she is discharged." Again, what? My mind spun out as I realized I had nowhere to take her if that happened. But of course, that hospice staff was so in tune with my feelings that when the charge nurse realized my state of shock at the possibility, she assured me there was no reason to worry about the next day. "Just trust things will be all right," she said. I had no other choice.

Day Six

Where is the food processor? I want to make some ham salad.

Am going to put someone to work painting fences. Where do you buy that Raider Red paint?

Life goes on.

Another strange consequence of the pandemic was a shift away from traditional funerals. At first, large gatherings were outright prohibited, leaving grieving spouses, parents, and children sitting alone at loved ones' services. But once things had settled down a bit, I think we all realized there were lots of different ways to honor someone's memory.

The hospice staff began gently raising questions about final arrangements. Mother wanted to be cremated—that much I knew. She had told me she did not want a service, but I remembered her saying, in the end, she didn't really care what we did because "dead is dead." I took that as permission to do what our family needed to process our grief, so I spent some time that day considering our options.

It was great therapy as I began writing out what a service in Mother's honor might look like. Our oldest son, John, is a minister, and I plugged him in as officiant, including his brothers in other ways. Where would we hold it? What would she wear? Would we wait until mask mandates were lifted and people could travel? A thousand questions kept my mind occupied during those long hours.

That evening, I sat with Mother, enjoying the idyllic scene from her window, listening quietly to Christian hymns, working a little, but mostly just mulling over things, enjoying the healing balm of God's Spirit. My mom rested peacefully under heavy sedation, seemingly unaware of her surroundings.

Day Seven

Hospice nurses are special—they have to be. As if dealing with the most advanced stages of countless diseases and providing comfort to a huge range of grieving friends and family members is not enough, they are proactive, with a special knack for anticipating the needs of the dying. That day, the nurse planned to bathe Mother, and I watched as she carefully dosed pain meds both before and after in order to keep her discomfort under control.

I never felt like I was alone. Doug, my boys and their wives, and countless friends of Mother's and mine checked in often. I knew we were being thought of and prayed for. Plus, the presence of the Lord was palpable in that place of sorrow.

It was a beautiful Texas day, so I ordered some delicious Mexican food and took my lunch outside. What happened next provided Doug and the kids with a good belly laugh when I sent this text:

> *If you picnic outside and a small green chameleon lizard confuses your leg for perhaps a tree trunk, any observers are sure to think you are being visited by the Holy Spirit. Especially in a place like this.*

Do they have security cameras where we can see the playback? my daughter-in-law quipped.

Life goes on.

Doug kept offering to come to Victoria, but due to some medication he was taking, I was afraid he would fall asleep at the wheel and give me another funeral to plan, so I asked him to stay home. He was working full-time in addition to doing the hard work of keeping farm life going—and making ham salad. Luke, our youngest, also kept telling me he wanted to come. Knowing he and his grandmother were never close, I did not want him to feel obligated to make the five-hundred-mile trip. His wife finally helped me realize he didn't want to be there because of her but because of me. Luke knew better than I did how much I actually could use a shoulder to cry on, and cry I did when he walked through the door the next day, enveloping me in his arms.

We realized that due to a combination of social distancing and Lutheran funeral regulations, we would not be able to have the service I had envisioned. My peace of mind about a memorial turned to utter frustration and uncertainty. In the end, we decided to run a nice obituary in the Port Lavaca newspaper, then later plan an outing to scatter her ashes. One of her favorite places on earth was Boot Canyon Trail in Big Bend National Park. Perhaps we could do it there.

I texted Doug, assuring him things were as good as they could be:

> *These past couple of days have been a time of reflection and healing. This is* her *final journey. When you reflect on what it all means, it is really a beautiful walk, a final, perfect spiritual journey, from this earth to her eternal home with Jesus. How can you not rejoice in knowing that?*
>
> *We walk by faith, not by sight. But when you hear someone who is dying roll call family members and call out to Jesus, that is a real-time confirmation of heaven.*

I sat with Mother all night, counting my blessings. I really believed she didn't have much longer.

Day Eight

Even with skilled intervention and care, dying is an ugly, horrible business. After a long night, that Friday, the doctor made his rounds and confirmed my feeling and the nurses' warnings that Mother was in her final days, if not hours. He said she was following "the textbook steps of dying." Leave it to Mother to check every box on her way out.

He did not believe she would be alive on Monday when he returned.

Day Nine

When I arrived the next morning, Mother's breathing had slowed and become shallower. The nurse prepared me for the likely eventuality the breaths would just stop without fanfare, like the final moments when the Energizer bunny bangs the drum for the last time. Luke sat vigil with me as messages of comfort and hope paraded through my mind: *No more sorrow, no more pain. When my work on earth is done. Faith is the victory. I can only imagine.*

The liminal space between life and death is grueling, and Luke and I were feeling its effects. I had been with Mother for so long that it would have broken my heart not to be present when she met the Lord, but Luke convinced me to get some sleep. He stayed at his grandmother's side that last night, watching over her as the angels drew near.

The Lord's Day

It was a glorious Sunday. The perfect day to go to heaven.

Mother's blood pressure had dropped overnight to 68/28, her oxygen level at a miserable 47 percent, her temperature spiked, and her heart beating more frantically. It had been days since she'd lost consciousness, and the nurse believed the final hours were close.

Although we had no doubt, it was then the Lord demonstrated that he was truly with us, paying attention to every detail and helping us realize he was near. For days, Luke and I had been enjoying the show of nature outside the lovely window in Mother's room. Redbirds flitted and danced in the trees, deer dotted the meadow leading to the creek, and the evening before, a skunk had sashayed down the path. It was a sanctuary, and Mother would have loved it. Around lunchtime, Luke and I both shot out of our chairs as we spotted an oversized bird with a long, white neck, black plumage, and a distinctive orange beak strutting past. Turns out, it was a northern crested caracara, parading around at the very northern edge of its normal territory. I just know this was a little token of comfort from God, the assurance his eye was on my mother in that place of death.

As the hours dragged on, she lingered. It's a strange sensation to struggle with the desire to see a loved one set free from pain, yet still wanting to absorb every remaining moment together, bottling the sights, sounds, smells, and touch of their hand while you can still be in the same place. Scripture continued to comfort me, especially Solomon's wisdom from Ecclesiastes 3:1–2a: "For everything there is a season, and a time for every matter under heaven: a time to be born, and a time to die."

The nurses graciously anticipated our needs, offering support without interfering in our private grief. When the time drew near, Luke and I were at Mother's bedside. Suddenly, her eyes, those emerald green pools that had guided me through life, popped open, seemingly by reflex. Luke gently reached over to close them, but she shook her head. If she was still conscious enough at that point, I wonder if it was her final, independent stand. But more likely, God had opened them, wanting her to enter eternity looking at his perfect, loving countenance, giving everyone in the room a glimpse into heaven as she took her final breath.

And suddenly, she was gone.

I have full confidence that, at that moment, she was present with the Lord, as the apostle Paul described in 2 Corinthians 5:8: "We are confident, I say, and willing rather to be absent from the body, and to be present with the Lord" (KJV).

Mother did not get to write the last chapter of her story, but, true to form, she penned the last paragraph. And even though Jesus was seemingly added in the final act, he had actually been there all along. I believe their sweet time together has just begun.

Epilogue

He heals the brokenhearted, and binds up their wounds.

—Psalm 147:3

WRITING THIS BOOK has forced me into a hard season of introspection. Some things I uncovered have been hurtful; others have made me sad. But it has been a healing process.

I hope these words provide a degree of hope and comfort for anyone who is going on a journey like ours. I also pray that the insights provide peace and understanding for my boys. As I reflect on my mother's life, I am overwhelmed at what I now believe was the hand of God at work in these situations. In a perfect world, that beautiful baby girl who came home with her parents would not have been abused, the sixteen-year-old would not have become pregnant, the sixty-nine-year-old would not have been living in fear for her future.

But God took it all, the whole ball of imperfection, and made it something worthy of Jesus's death.

For the last four years, I have pondered what Mother meant when she instructed me to "finish the book, get it published." I truly had no idea where that thought originated. Was it from the final conversation we had in her home where I said we don't always get to write the final chapter of our story? In her confused mental state, some six months later, is this the book she was referring to? Or was God putting the command in her mind to plant the seed in me, in a sense saying, "There is a story here that is about to unfold that needs to be told"?

During the writing process, I reached out to one of Mother's coworkers at the shelter. When I mentioned the book, she and I both paused in wonder: Fellow shelter volunteers had told my mom for years that between her travel adventures and strong opinions, she had at least one book in her just waiting to be written. We agreed that the fact Mother never got to write the book and now I was doing it was amazing. I don't know that I produced the book she would've written—as a matter of fact, I know I did not—but I think she would have approved, especially regarding the ending. Especially if her story encourages even one other person to say, "Sign me up!"

As I hope I've communicated well throughout this story, my husband's compassionate support has buoyed me along. To him, writing Mother's story was an act of obedience. God had given me a task and even though I hadn't fully realized the implications (and still don't), I had agreed to "write the book." He consistently stormed heaven's gates on behalf of the message before it was even fully formed.

When I first told him of my desire to put pen to paper, he didn't hesitate to support and encourage me. Cost didn't matter. Time away from him didn't matter. He could see God guiding me to craft this tale and didn't want to be party to any disobedience. While reflecting on the process the other day, Doug once again affirmed that every painful memory, every hard truth unearthed, every minute invested digging through boxes of photos and newspaper clippings had been worth it.

As I sat at the keyboard recounting the final days of my mom's life, those dark yet hopeful hours that seemed they would have no end, he took my hand and once again imbued me with the strength to continue typing. "If your mother's story leads one single person to Christ," he said, "then this was all worth it."

Amen and amen. Come soon, Lord Jesus.

Jesus's Parable of the Vineyard Laborers, Matthew 20:1–16

For the kingdom of heaven is like a householder who went out early in the morning to hire laborers for his vineyard. After agreeing with the laborers for a denarius a day, he sent them into his vineyard. And going out about the third hour he saw others standing idle in the market place and to them he said, "You go into the vineyard too, and whatever is right I will give you." So they went. Going out again about the sixth hour and the ninth hour, he did the same. And about the eleventh hour he went out and found others standing; and he said to them, "Why do you stand here idle all day?"

They said to him, "Because no one has hired us."

He said to them, "You go into the vineyard too." And when evening came, the owner of the vineyard said to his steward, 'Call the laborers and pay them their wages, beginning with the last, up to the first." And when those hired about the eleventh hour came, each of them received a denarius.

Now when the first came, they thought they would receive more; but each of them also received a denarius. And on receiving it they grumbled at the householder, saying, "These last worked only one hour, and you have made them equal to us who have borne the burden of the day and the scorching heat."

But he replied to one of them, "Friend, I am doing you no wrong; did you not agree with me for a denarius? Take what belongs to you, and go; I choose to give to this last as I give to you. Am I not allowed to do what I choose with what belongs to me? Or do you begrudge my generosity? So the last will be first, and the first last."

Acknowledgments

There have been so many people who have encouraged me to "write the book," I don't think they realize the role they played or, more importantly, how God used them to bring this to fruition.

My family: Doug, John, Paul, Samantha, Adelyn, Audrey, Luke, Lacey, Laken, Lily, and Linkin. Thank you for providing me with the love and support I needed not only to get through those last days with Mother but to continue to live in the love and forgiveness Christ offers us all.

My friend Halie, who said, "Oh my gosh, Allison, you have to share this story," reminded me of the promise I made to my mother at the very beginning of those long and difficult last ten days. That promise had gotten lost in all that was happening.

My friend Evans, who was obedient to God's call and placed that call to me and listened to the story while I was driving some two hours to Abilene, Texas. He began encouraging me and even pushing me a bit to tell this story. As I have shared with him, I truly believe that God was laying the foundation of this story to be told when he brought Evans and my son John together as friends and fellow students of ministry at Columbia International University. I do not imagine any other person could have called me out of the blue and ultimately earned my trust to "Finish the book. Get it published."

But most of all, to my new dear friend Traci. She has been more than my editor. She was my counselor, gently encouraging me to open doors that I did not want to open. To dig deep into my memories and thoughts. I knew that my mother's story was deep and complex, but, in the end, it had a poetic beauty that needed to be painted with the written word. Traci, it has been my greatest privilege to work with you, and I think, together, we have created something good. You have been everything I hoped for but more than I could have imagined. *May the Lord bless you and keep you; the Lord make his face shine upon you and be gracious to you; the Lord lift up his countenance upon you and give you peace* (Numbers 6:24–26).

About the Author

Allison Crabtree is a Christ follower who lives nearly off the grid with her husband on their Texas farm, enjoying both the work involved and the peace and quiet of country living. Like her mother did, she spends inordinate amounts of time sewing and wielding a crochet hook. A graduate of both Texas A&M and Texas Tech, Allison earned the title of professional engineer (PE) and has been a pioneer in that male-dominated field. Mother of three boys (now men, but always "her boys"), she currently enjoys the title of Granny to Laken, Adelyn, Lily, Audrey, and Linkin more than any previous moniker.

Allison is available to share her story and message of hope with any groups that would like to hear.

She can be reached at signmeupjesus@gmail.com.

www.ingramcontent.com/pod-product-compliance
Lightning Source LLC
Chambersburg PA
CBHW020241010526
44107CB00039B/1460/J